GOD AND STARBUCKS

GOD AND STARBUCKS

An NBA Superstar's Journey

Through Addiction and Recovery

VIN BAKER

with Joe Layden

Amistad

An Imprint of HarperCollins*Publishers*

GOD AND STARBUCKS. Copyright © 2017 by Vin Baker. All rights reserved. Printed in the United States of America. No part of this book may be used or reproduced in any manner whatsoever without written permission except in the case of brief quotations embodied in critical articles and reviews. For information, address HarperCollins Publishers, 195 Broadway, New York, NY 10007.

HarperCollins books may be purchased for educational, business, or sales promotional use. For information, please e-mail the Special Markets Department at SPsales@harpercollins.com.

FIRST EDITION

Designed by Michelle Crowe

Library of Congress Cataloging-in-Publication Data has been applied for.

ISBN 978-0-06-249681-2

17 18 19 20 21   LSC   10 9 8 7 6 5 4 3 2 1

*This book is dedicated to my wonderful mother, Jean Baker;
my wife and partner, Shawnee; my father (and pastor),
James, who never gave up on me; and God,
who always sees the best in me!*

You never know God is all you need until God is all you have.

—RICK WARREN

CONTENTS

★ ★ ★

INTRODUCTION

I can see it on their faces sometimes. They walk into the store, heavy lidded, distracted by thoughts of the upcoming workday, looking for nothing more than a jolt of caffeine to shake off the morning cobwebs. They peck away at their smartphones or fumble with their wallets, oblivious to their surroundings, until suddenly, there they are, at the front of the line, looking up—way up—at the world's tallest barista.

Some feign cool indifference, but most can't help themselves. I grew up in Connecticut, played college ball at the University of Hartford, and spent part of my career—a rather notorious part—with the Boston Celtics. So here, at a Starbucks in North Kingstown, Rhode Island, there's no place to hide. First of all, I don't look like an ordinary guy. I'm a giant in the back there. I mean that literally—I'm six foot eleven, 275 pounds. You see me frothing up your cappuccino, and at the very least you can't help but wonder, *What's going on here? He must be . . . somebody.* Others know exactly who I am: a guy who made, and lost, more than $100 million in his NBA career, a career wrecked by alcoholism and depression and spectacularly bad business decisions. These are the people who stare hard, then suddenly avert their eyes, the sadness nevertheless evident on their faces.

I know what they're thinking: How the hell does a four-time NBA all-star, and an Olympian, end up shouting "Tall decaf cappuccino!" from behind the counter at Starbucks? Given half the chance, I'll disarm the customer with a smile and a few friendly words. I don't want anyone to feel uncomfortable when they walk into our store, and I sure don't want anyone's pity. Trust me when I say this: I've been through worse. Much, much worse. There's no shame in work. The indignity comes from not working, from losing your way through ego and weakness and addiction, and finding yourself tumbling into a bottomless pit of despair and helplessness.

Want to know what that looks like? Okay, here it is.

I was a first-round NBA draft pick (the eighth choice overall in 1993) smoking weed every day to alleviate my anxiety, until repeated trips to the emergency room, with my heart racing uncontrollably, prompted me to find another way to self-medicate.

I was an NBA all-star, drinking after games, and then before games, and eventually at all points in between—draining anywhere between a pint and a fifth of liquor a day—using alcohol to end my career and nearly my life. Make no mistake, that's what alcoholism is: slow and deliberate suicide.

I was a man running from responsibility, fathering five children with two different women, and selfishly bouncing back and forth between families and relationships, because money gave me leeway and freedom that others were not afforded. Money, after all, is like a "get out of jail free" card—until it's gone, and with it the patience and tolerance of those you've hurt, and the enabling of those who never really cared about you in the first place.

I was a former millionaire driving my mother's Mercedes (the one I bought her with my rookie contract) to a pawnshop, with four old tires stuffed into the backseat and trunk. I sold the tires for eighty bucks, bought a few bottles of liquor, and drank myself into oblivion, until all the pain was gone—the ache in my lower back that signaled a failing liver, and the ceaseless cloud of loneliness that hung over every day.

That's how bad it got for me.

By comparison, working at Starbucks is a walk in the park.

Would you prefer to say that I got my ass kicked? That I've been humbled? Fine, go ahead and say it. You would not be incorrect. But I'm not bitter. I've been sober for six years now, and in that time, with spirituality as the foundation, I've rebuilt my life one brick at a time. I married a longtime girlfriend, and together we are raising our four beautiful children. I am a licensed minister and assistant pastor at the same church in Old Saybrook, Connecticut, where my father is the head pastor, and where, as a boy, I knew nothing but peace. I'll probably never be a millionaire again, but that's fine. Life is good and full of possibilities.

That's the point I'd like to get across: that life is worth living, no matter how bad it might get at times. Obstacles can be overcome, demons can be conquered. I've been speaking to youth groups both in and out of church, and I've done some work with the NBA, helping provide a cautionary tale to young athletes who likely aren't even remotely prepared for the ways in which their lives will change when staggering wealth is heaped on them. This book is part of my mission. Maybe, by telling my story, I can provide inspiration and hope to those who are facing all manner of hardships, and who are trying to figure out how to pick themselves up and start over again.

As I tell the parishioners at my church: God doesn't measure how far you've fallen, but he will be there when you're ready to rise.

GOD AND STARBUCKS

PROLOGUE

APRIL 16, 2011

This day begins like all the others, like every gray and god-forsaken morning for the previous seven months: with a feeling of utter astonishment that I am still alive. There is no relief attached to this sentiment, no gratitude, just a sense of wonder at how much the human body can withstand before it finally surrenders or gives out. I roll over on the couch, which is where I usually sleep, and squint out at the bleakness of another day rising up to taunt me. As I sit up, the pounding in my head starts almost immediately, followed by heart palpitations and epic, rumbling waves of nausea. I begin to tremble and sweat. I am dizzy and disoriented.

If this sounds like a hangover—well, that doesn't even begin to do it justice. Hangovers are for rookies. I am a veteran, a world-class drinker and drug addict who spends his every waking moment trying to dull the pain of a hopelessly wrecked life. What I feel right now is not a mere hangover; it is a body in the throes of withdrawal. The alcoholic drinks all day, passes out at night, and wakes to a craving that can scarcely be described—an immediate awareness that agony lies ahead, and the only way to stop it is to take the first drink. There is nothing surprising about any of this to me, not anymore. I know the routine and have planned accordingly. On the coffee table in front of me is a small portion of an orange, peeled and ready to be eaten, along with a jug of Hennessy and an empty glass. Although I don't remember doing so, at some point the previous night I laid these items out on the table, knowing they would be needed the moment I woke up. And there they are, ready to be applied like some alcoholic's balm.

I reach first for the Hennessy, of course. Pour a small amount in the glass, maybe three or four ounces, take a deep breath, and toss it back. There is a familiar burning sensation, at once soothing and aggravating. Then I put the glass down and reach for the orange. Sometimes I try to eat the entire piece; on this day I am just too sick, so I squeeze some of the juice into my mouth, try to swallow, and then wait for the inevitable. I reach out, grab a small waste can (also kept nearby at all times), and vomit the meager contents of my stomach—a mix of blood and bile, mostly—into the bottom. The spasms go on for a minute or two, dry heaving so powerfully that my ribs feel as though they are compressed against my spine. Whimpering softly, I fall back into the couch and curl up into a ball. In a few minutes I will begin to feel better. The sweat will dissipate, the headache will subside, and the fog will begin to lift.

And then I can begin to drink in earnest.

That's the way it usually works. On this day, though, the sickness lingers. There is a persistent pain in my lower back; it's been there for a while now, increasing steadily in severity, a sure sign that my liver is beginning to fail. I rise from the couch, pull a blanket around me, and stagger through darkened rooms. I grew up in this house, and right now it is all I have left. Gone are the mansions and the cars and most of the friends who came with them. My parents live nearby, in a home that I bought for them many years ago, when I was flush with fame and fortune. We never sold my childhood home, so I've moved back in. I guess this is what is known as coming full circle, although I don't recall my parents ever having to worry about the cable company killing service for nonpayment, as happened to me not long ago.

At the moment I have five children, but I rarely see any of them. Truth is, I hardly see anyone. I've burned just about every available bridge over the last decade, and so most days are spent right here, in this living room, completely alone, drinking as much as a gallon of Hennessy every single day. That's the beverage of choice right now, no better or worse than the Bacardi 151 I used to drink, or even the Listerine I once favored as a way to get drunk without smelling like a drunk. As always, on this morning, I am amazed to be drawing breath.

I can't believe I made it through another night.

Maybe there is a reason God hasn't called me yet. There was a time, after all, when he was the most important person in my life. Long before I became an NBA all-star, long before I made and lost more money than most people can even imagine, I lived a life of humility and spirituality. I was the son of a preacher, and even when I lost my way, I liked to think of myself as still being part of the flock. It was always back there somewhere, the idea that I was the prodigal son, just waiting for a chance to go home.

I make my way to the bathroom, turn on the lights, and catch a glimpse of myself in the mirror. Most days I turn away from my own reflection, because what I see disgusts and frightens me. Gone is the world-class athlete with an easy and ever-present smile; in his place is a sad and sick man in the final stages of a death spiral. This is what end-stage alcoholism looks like: yellow, sunken eyes, hollow cheeks, 190 pounds of sagging, wrinkled flesh draped across a six-foot-eleven frame. In my playing days I carried 250 pounds of muscle. Now I am a living, breathing skeleton. A walking corpse.

For some reason, I stare at the reflection, unable or unwilling to avert my gaze. Every inch of my body aches. Not just a superficial pain, but something much deeper and more primal. I feel it in my bones. I feel it in my heart. I feel it in my soul, which is a surprise, since I wasn't even sure that particular part of me still existed. This is bottom. Finally, after all these years, this is it.

I begin to cry, almost silently at first, and then much louder—full-throated sobs that take my breath away. I fall to my knees and, for the first time in many years, I begin to pray. It is a selfish prayer, a plea for relief more than forgiveness.

"Please, God . . . take this away from me. I can't do it anymore."

There is no response, of course. Just more pain and despair. That's okay—God is a busy man, and you can't blame him for wanting to see some evidence of sincerity before extending the hand of salvation. I rise from the floor and walk into the living room. I pick up my cell phone and punch in the number of one of the few people who will still take my call, the one person who will give me another chance, no matter what I've done, or how far I have fallen.

"Dad," I whisper into the phone. "I'm ready to check in to rehab. Will you help me?"

He's there in minutes, and soon the two of us are on the road, my father behind the wheel, me slumped into the passenger seat, sipping from a bottle of Hennessy (as any addict will tell you, if you're going to rehab, you might as well get high on the way; go out with a bang, so to speak). We barely talk. There isn't much to say. My father is a hard man, but he is a forgiving man as well. Like everyone else, my parents have kept me at arm's length for a while now. At some point, there is nothing you can do for the addict but give him the time and space to make his own decisions, and hope that he eventually chooses life over death. For me, that day is today. I am forty-one years old, and I am leaning on my father like a child.

He walks me to the front door of the hospital. There are no tears, no words of wisdom. He simply extends his hand for me to shake. I take it in mine and pull him close.

"I love you, Dad."

"I love you, too, son. Good luck."

1

★ ★ ★

GROWING UP

I am not one of those people who can blame their adult problems on an impoverished or abusive childhood. My mother and father left the South during the turbulent sixties, settled in the more tolerant and integrated Northeast, and raised a family. I grew up an only child; there was another baby, born three years before me, but he passed away because of health issues before I came along. In part because of the emotional trauma attached to that event, but also because my folks were just old fashioned, I was raised in a loving but strict environment, and kept on a very short leash. If my parents didn't approve of one of my friends, then I wasn't allowed to spend time with that friend. I had strict curfews.

Both of my parents worked, my mom as a quality-control

operator at the Cheesbrough-Ponds cosmetics company, my father as a mechanic and a minister. Old Saybrook is not a racially diverse community, and I was one of the few African American kids at my school. But my life revolved around a Baptist church (more like Pentecostal, really), with a predominantly black congregation, so I kind of felt like I had the best of both worlds. My father was a bad boy turned good. Drank too much, ran the streets, then turned his life around. With a streetwise father like that, there's no way a kid gets away with much. My parents understood racism and the potential problems of being a black kid in a white town; they also knew firsthand what sort of trouble a kid could find if he was allowed to roam free.

So I didn't roam. I went to school and church. I did my homework. I stayed out of trouble. By any reasonable definition, I was a good kid.

What I wasn't, at least not for a while, was a good basketball player. I was a classic late bloomer: six foot two and skeletal as a ninth-grader, I got cut from the varsity and the JV. I loved the game, but the fact is, my physical development lagged far behind my enthusiasm. I wasn't big enough or strong enough to bang inside, and my handle was too weak for point guard, the position I'd played in eighth grade. Like most kids who get cut, I went home and cried to my parents, who were thoroughly disengaged from youth sports and really couldn't comprehend my disappointment. Mom worked the second shift (4:00 p.m. to 1:00 a.m), and Dad was at church all the time. They were too busy to get caught up in their kid's high school sports drama. There were more important things to worry about.

Sorry, son. Maybe next year. Now go do your homework.

But in the off-season I worked hard, continued to play,

and didn't feel sorry for myself but rather used getting cut as motivation. I wanted to prove to the coaches that they had made a mistake. Besides, I loved hoopin'. Couldn't get enough of it. I wasn't the biggest or toughest kid, but I was passionate about the game, and that goes a long way. While other kids moved from one sport to another depending on the time of year, I focused exclusively on basketball. Like a lot of kids, I dreamed of one day making it to the NBA; unlike most kids, I devoted all my energy to making it happen, regardless of whether it was a realistic goal. Somewhere between the ages of thirteen and sixteen, most boys develop interests that challenge their devotion to sports. In my case the transition was delayed by several years. All I needed to be happy was a ball and a gym. I was a decent student—not high honors or anything, but solid enough to stay out of trouble. I didn't party or stay out late. I just played ball and went to school and church. All day, every day.

Good thing I was patient and determined, because I was far from an overnight success. Even in my sophomore year, things didn't pop right away. I was a six-three wing still relegated to the JV. One game, after scoring 20 points, I felt pretty good about myself, and kind of swaggered into the locker room as the varsity was getting ready to come out. As I passed one of the older guys I gave myself a little shout-out, just to let him know that I was a baller.

"Dropped twenty tonight," I said.

He shook his head. "Whatever, Bako" (my nickname). "You're on the JV."

True enough. And until I proved otherwise, that's all I was.

Genetics trumps almost everything, though. My father was a drinker. A couple of my uncles, too. I was predisposed to alcoholism. But my dad was also six foot seven, so I inherited the tall gene as well. You take the good with the bad, I guess. I had my first legitimate growth spurt near the end of my sophomore year, and by the time I started school as a junior, my father and I were the same height. Of course, he outweighed me by a hundred pounds and still scared the hell out of me, but the added size did wonders for my confidence, as well as for my basketball game. The other thing that helped was competition. The whole summer before my junior year, I played two or three times a week at the YMCA in Westbrook, Connecticut. These were grown-up games dominated by current and former college players and playground legends. At first it was hard to get into the games, but I waited my turn, and once given a chance, I moved the ball, played hard on defense, and kept my mouth shut. Respect came slowly but steadily, and pretty soon I was a regular. My father would drop me off at six and pick me up at eight. For two hours I'd get my butt kicked, and then go home. Dad rarely even asked me about those games, but I think he approved. He wasn't an athlete, but he liked the idea that I was showing some initiative.

I also went to a camp that summer at the University of Connecticut. Recruiting was different in those days; not everyone played AAU ball, and certainly it didn't dominate the recruiting landscape the way it does today. A lot of kids were recruited based on their high school performance, or by playing well at a particular camp. It didn't occur to me that I could play at UConn, or any other program at the elite level of Division I. But the competition was fierce at this camp, and I liked it. I was skinny and slow, lumbered around a little, trying to figure out my new body, but I didn't back down. Even when I was getting pushed around and guys were dunking in my face, I liked playing. I knew the competition would make me better, and I wanted as much of it as I could get. I didn't have a game plan. I wasn't a blue-chip recruit with a street agent and free sneakers. It's not like I got cut in ninth grade and said, "One day I'll be an Olympian." I was just a wiry kid from Old Saybrook who liked playing basketball so much that he couldn't imagine quitting. Eventually my body began to catch up with my enthusiasm, but at times it felt like a glacial process.

Complicating matters was the fact that I was a young black man in a predominantly (almost exclusively) white community, so I lived something of a double life. At home, at church, and on the playgrounds, I was surrounded by African Americans. At Old Saybrook High School, however, I was one of only a small number of black males. My parents were from the South and had come of age during the civil rights era. From them, and from other parishioners at our church, I heard stories of segregation and oppression, and while I experienced nothing quite that severe while growing up, I did see black and white very clearly. I experienced racism and bigotry on a more subtle level, but I did feel its sting, and I never forgot it. And I used it as a motivational tool.

There was a kid my age at Old Saybrook named Aaron Smith. He transferred in as a freshman (we had played against each other in eighth grade) and immediately became the star of the program. Aaron was a big, strong white kid, more physically advanced than I was, and certainly a lot tougher than I was. At that point in our lives, there is no question that Aaron was a better basketball player than me, and everyone knew it. He was elevated to the varsity as a freshman, while I couldn't even make the JV. This had nothing to do with the color of our skin, but I had trouble looking at things objectively. I was angry with Aaron, and I was envious of him. I was so angry that I quit the freshman team—just walked off with two weeks left in the season. I would look at Aaron and see him living the life of a varsity player, while I couldn't even make the JV, and I would seethe with anger and frustration.

So I quit. And then I decided that quitting wasn't the answer; hard work was the answer.

Aaron and I both attended the UConn camp after tenth grade. It was a very competitive camp with a lot of college coaches in attendance. Suddenly I started to get some buzz. Part of this was a natural result of my physical maturation. There was talent and size to go along with the tension and anger, and college recruiters began to take notice. The first step in the recruiting process, after all, is to pass the eye test—to *look* like a player. I had no idea how to put it all together, but for the first time I discovered that channeling my emotion in the right way could be beneficial. Simply put: when I played angry, I played better. But in a very real sense, I felt like I was on my own. The coaching staff didn't believe in me, my parents didn't believe in me (or didn't care, because basketball simply wasn't all that important to them), my teammates didn't believe in me. At least that's the way I felt in my sixteen-year-old head. I had something to prove.

Aaron and I were expected to be the two best players on the team our junior year, and we got along okay for the most part, until something happened during the preseason workouts. Aaron had a pickup truck, and he was driving around gathering everyone for the workout one afternoon. At one point I volunteered to jump in the back because the truck's cab was becoming uncomfortably crowded.

"Just give me a second," I said as we pulled out of the driveway. "I'll climb into the back."

Before I had even settled into the bed of the truck, Aaron

punched the accelerator—hard. I went flying off the back of the truck and broke my fall with my arm. I knew right away that something bad had happened. The pain was severe and instantaneous. Even worse, when I fell off the truck my pants caught on the edge of the truck bed, so I was literally dragged down the street for about five seconds, screaming at the top of my lungs, before anyone knew what had happened. When the truck came to a stop, the response was not exactly compassionate.

"My bad," Aaron said as he jumped out of the truck. "Didn't know you weren't ready."

This may have been true, but the fact that Aaron was laughing as he said it really bothered me. Not only that, but as the shock of the incident wore off, I realized that I had probably seriously injured my arm.

"Dude, look at this," I said, holding up my wrist, which was bent at an odd angle. "I've never had a broken bone before, but I'm pretty sure this is messed up."

The pain was bad enough, and my wrist twisted at such a weird angle, that we decided to cancel our workout. Instead, we went to another friend's house and watched TV. By the time I got home that evening my arm was throbbing.

"I think I need to go to the emergency room," I said. "It really hurts."

My parents were not the coddling type, but as they watched me squirm while trying to flex my wrist, they became concerned. Dad drove me to the hospital, where X-rays confirmed my fears: I had a broken wrist. When the doctor told me that the fracture would require roughly two months to heal, I felt my heart sink. This was early October; the start of basketball season was only a few weeks away. Depending on how quickly the bone healed, I could miss several games.

I was devastated, and one of the first things I did when I got home was call my buddies to commiserate. I called Aaron first, and his response took me aback.

"It's broken, dude," I said. "Can you believe it?"

There was silence on the other end of the line, a long pause before Aaron finally spoke.

"Awww, that's too bad, man."

And that was it. He didn't apologize, didn't express any real emotion. Looking back on this now as an adult, I understand that he might have felt awkward or embarrassed or otherwise responsible for what happened, and as a sixteen-year-old simply wasn't capable of expressing contrition. But something about that conversation did not feel right. We were teammates, if not exactly friends; we were the two best players on the team, but my impending absence did not seem to bother him. Maybe he didn't want to have to share the spotlight. Or perhaps, it could have been something deeper. This is a hard thing to convey without sounding alarmist, or being accused of playing the race card, but when you're a black kid in a white world, sometimes you just feel things; you know in your gut that something isn't quite right. Do I think that Aaron tried to hurt me because I was black and he was white? No, it's not that simple or that blatant.

From that moment on, I vowed that Aaron would never be better than me on a basketball court. This was going to be personal from here on out. I would work within the team concept and treat him, as I did all teammates, with respect, but I would be competing against him as well as with him.

It's me against you, buddy.

I kept this mostly to myself; it wasn't like I had a bunch of black friends with whom I could share my suspicions or frustrations. I tried to talk with my parents about it, but they felt like I was overreacting, or reaching for something that wasn't there. To their eyes, my broken wrist was merely the result of bad adolescent driving. It happened. Nothing personal. I saw things differently, and I had a hard time letting go of those feelings. Maybe that wasn't such a bad thing, for they fueled a rage that drove me to be successful, to prove people wrong, and to rise above my surroundings.

The basketball court became my sanctuary, a place where I could forget about my problems, a place where I wasn't anxious all the time and unsure of myself, as I often was in social situations or at school. Anxiety is a terrible affliction, and I had suffered from it as far back as I could remember. It made me extraordinarily nervous, to the point where I would sometimes feel the urge to be invisible, to just disappear, so that no one would expect anything of me. On the court, however, I was confident and strong. I believed in myself.

My wrist healed on schedule, and while I missed a few practices, I was back in time for the first game. As a junior, I averaged about 16 points per game, which was pretty good, but not enough to attract any serious interest from college coaches. If I had been playing today, the path would have been different. I would have played AAU ball in the spring and summer, and someone would have noticed that I was a late bloomer and shipped me off to prep school for an extra year of seasoning (i.e., physical maturation and intense academic support). The paradigm of college sports in America has shifted dramatically since I was a kid. Today it's not unusual for parents to hold their child back a year and start kindergarten at age six. The promising athlete then picks up a redshirt year along the way, and now the twenty-year-old college freshman is fairly common.

By comparison, I was seventeen when I started my senior

year. Thanks to respectable performances in a couple of preseason tournaments, combined with another growth spurt that left me at a legitimate six foot eleven, the phone began to ring. Not heavily, mind you, but there were offers. The University of Hartford, a fledgling D-1 program just an hour or so from home, was the first to reach out, and the most persistent in its pursuit. I was flattered by the attention and I liked the idea of being part of a new program. True, it wasn't UConn or Duke or Syracuse, but schools at that level had expressed no interest in me, and that wasn't going to change. In the parlance of the game, I was a "project," a kid who had developed late and might, with a little luck and lots of hard work, continue to develop. The big schools didn't have time to invest in projects. There was too much at stake.

That was fine with me. I liked the Hartford coach, Jack Phelan (although, like all coaches, he would prove to be much less cuddly in the gym than he was on the recruiting trail). I liked the guys on the team. I liked the campus. And I really liked my recruiting visit. See, it wasn't so much what Hartford had to offer that turned my head. Eventually all the good stuff came: playing time, professional opportunities, small classes, and strong relationships with faculty and teammates, everything that had been pitched. But what really sold me on Hartford was the pretty girl who agreed to dance with me at my first college party. Simple, right? But completely true. I was a naive high school senior who, basketball camp aside, had never been away from home overnight on his own, and who had never been to a party. At the time, this was the best night of my life. By the end of the weekend, I was ready to sign with Hartford. It didn't happen right away, though. For a while I flirted with the University of Rhode Island, but they never made a formal offer and eventually my mother shook some sense into me.

"You'd better take this scholarship before they give it to someone else," she said. "You can't afford to miss this opportunity."

I called Coach Phelan and committed. I don't even think I was his top recruit. We had seven freshmen on the team—that's the way it works when you're building a program from scratch. I didn't care. I'd played only a single season of high school varsity basketball and already I'd earned a college scholarship. It didn't bother me in the least that I was going to a small school with a brand-new Division I program. And in retrospect, I realize that if I had gone to a top-tier program, I may not have developed into the player I became. Some kids thrive in an intensely competitive environment, sink or swim. Others need more reassurance. I fell into the latter group, and as a result I am a strong proponent of being a big fish in a little pond. There's value in that. For example, I believe that the best player in the world right now would not be the best player in the world if he hadn't gone to Davidson. There, at a small college, playing for a mid-major program that had never known national success, Stephen Curry was able to explore different facets of his game; he was able to learn and to grow, and to play through his mistakes.

Steph was clearly Davidson's best player. When you're just one of ten—at Kentucky, for example, or any other big school—you're constantly struggling for playing time and fighting for respect. You could be one of the top ten players in your class when you arrive on campus, and in October you'll find yourself hosting a high school recruit who is ranked even higher in his class, and who will be after your job the following year. It's enormously intense and competitive. Every practice, every drill, is like a test. You can't just coast on talent the way you could in high school, because you are surrounded by players who are at least as talented, and perhaps more ambitious. If you relax for even one moment, you can get your ass kicked in a very public way. The potential for embarrassment is always present, every single day. Not everyone is built for that kind of pressure. I honestly believe that if you had dropped me on the University of Connecticut's campus—which is basically a small city—when I was eighteen years old, I wouldn't have survived. I could not have handled the pressure that came with being a UConn Husky in that era (a time when the program was a powerhouse member of a powerhouse conference—the Big East). Actually, I'm not even sure I could have found my way from my dorm to the gym, or to my classes.

It would have been a disaster.

But at cozy little Hartford? I'd be right at home. Or so I thought.

2

★ ★ ★

BIG FISH, LITTLE POND

As it turned out, I couldn't have been less prepared for the reality of being a college freshman. In the dorm and on the basketball court, I was a fish out of water. When I showed up for orientation in September, I didn't even have any luggage. I was so clueless as to what this experience would be like that I didn't even realize I'd be living there full time. My whole life had revolved around school and basketball and spending time with my parents. For better or worse, I was a momma's boy. A few hours after I was dropped off, I had to call my parents and ask them to bring me some sheets for my bed and some clothes. The enormity of it all was overwhelming, so much so that I became one of those sad and homesick freshmen who hop on the bus and go home every weekend.

The irony, of course, is that I couldn't wait to go to college and to get away from the rules my parents had imposed. But I was so accustomed to being with them and living under their tight jurisdiction that freedom scared the living daylights out of me. People kept coming in and out of my dorm room—without even knocking! Inviting me to go out!

You mean I can leave and go across campus? On my own? No, thanks. Forget it. I'm good. I'll just stay here. Matter of fact, I think I'm going home.

Basketball saved me, although it wasn't easy. I struggled mightily my freshman year. I cried—literally cried, with tears streaming down my face—two or three times a week in practice, and out of practice. Coach Phelan was one of those legitimately tough guys who held nothing back. He was a Hartford native who had played college ball at Saint Francis (Pennsylvania) and was a sixth-round draft pick of the Golden State Warriors. Although he never played in the NBA, Jack was a very good player who was probably destined to become a coach. He was smart and demanding and worked his butt off. And he expected the same of everyone who played for him. No excuses were permitted, and volatility was normal.

He was a lot like my mom, actually: very tough and exacting, and so emotional that sometimes you couldn't hear the message behind the rant. My father was big and intimidating, and once or twice he put a whipping on me when I was growing up, but generally speaking he was the calmer, cooler presence in our house. Mom was the screamer; so was Coach Phelan.

Interestingly, as much as I hated being the target of his outbursts, I can't deny that Coach Phelan had a positive impact on my basketball career and my life. In fact, if I had to pinpoint one coach who flipped the switch for me and got me into the pro realm—who convinced me that I could make a living as a basketball player—it was Jack Phelan. He challenged me. He got in my face. Now, admittedly, that doesn't always work. My high school coach was relatively soft, so I'd never been exposed to anyone like Coach Phelan. Fortunately, I'd had my hair blown back by my mother on more than one occasion, so Jack just sort of took her place when I got to college. I'm not saying it was easy. As much as I loved basketball, there were days I hated going to practice because I knew I was going to get chewed out in front of everyone. Coach Phelan saw something in me that I didn't even see in myself, and he figured this was the way to pull it out. But it was such a painful, uphill battle. I'd leave practice some days shaking my head, eyes bloodshot from crying, wondering whether I was wasting my time.

"Baker!" Coach Phelan yelled one day, in the middle of what I'm sure he considered to be a particularly disappointing practice performance. "Get over here."

I lowered my head and walked slowly to the edge of the court, where Jack stood waiting, arms folded across his chest, face contorted into a mask of disgust. I stopped a couple of feet short of him, but he quickly closed the gap. He leaned into me. I was a head taller than Jack, but felt somehow smaller in his presence. At that point in my life, he intimidated the hell out of me.

"You know what?" he said, his voice suddenly quieter, which had the odd effect of being even more unsettling. "I don't know if you're good enough to play here." There was a long pause as he prepared to deliver the kill shot. "In fact,

I don't even know if you're good enough to play on our women's team."

He stood there for a moment, letting the words sink in, probably waiting to see if I would give it back, waiting for me to demonstrate something resembling toughness. Instead, as my eyes welled with tears, I looked right through him. I could see my teammates and coaches just a few feet away, watching and listening, but feigning indifference. This was still relatively early in the season, so I wondered what they thought of me. Coach Phelan picked on everyone, but I was rapidly becoming a favorite target. And my response, fostered while I was growing up, was one of naked emotion. At Old Saybrook High School people knew that I was passionate because they dealt with me on a daily basis.

Passionate.

That's the way I like to think of it. Sounds better than "immature" or "hypersensitive" or "soft." I was passionate on the basketball court; I was passionate about my game. I was passionate about school and friendships and life. As a result, coaches and teachers had given me a wide berth sometimes. They treated me gently. Now, though, I was an eighteen-year-old college freshman thrown into the meat grinder of Division I athletics. Even at the mid-major level, there is a sink-or-swim approach to college basketball; this was especially true a quarter century ago. Sensitivity was not high on any coach's priority list. Jack knew that I had talent but questioned my heart and probably my work ethic. Tactically, his approach to dealing with my shortcomings was rooted in old-school, militaristic wisdom: break him down, build him back up. I understand the logic; it's worked with countless athletes over the years, and eventually it worked with me. But, man . . . was it a struggle. As I blinked back tears, I could see the disappointment on Jack's face. I could almost hear his thoughts:

Seriously, Baker? You're crying again?

Jack didn't understand that the tears were the result of anger, not weakness. I was pissed off. There were tears, yes, and that's all anybody seemed to notice, but if they had looked at my body language, they would have seen the rigidity, the tight back, and the hands balled into fists. The tears indicated softness and a propensity for quitting, but the body language said, *I'm getting ready to do something to somebody and I'm not even exactly sure what it's going to be.*

I survived Jack Phelan's version of boot camp, though just barely. Trust me—if you were to have looked at me as a college freshman, averaging a measly 4.9 points and eleven minutes per game playing in one of the weakest conferences in college basketball, you never would have imagined that I'd end up being a productive college player, let alone a top-ten NBA draft pick. But opportunities came my way, and I tried to make the most of them.

First, in the summer of 1990, after my freshman year, I was invited to take part in an overseas trip on a team composed entirely of North Atlantic Conference (NAC) all-stars. Now, I wasn't an all-star. Not even close. But Jack was coaching the team, and he got to pick two of his own players. Our leading scorer, Lamont Middleton, had transferred to Saint John's, and another player turned down the offer. So Coach Phelan invited me. Training camp would be at Hartford over the summer, he explained, a couple of weeks before we left. There would be games in Finland and Sweden. Good competition, good chance for growth, Jack explained. But it would be hard. He made that point clear.

"No problem, Coach," I said. "I'll be there."

The NAC would never be confused with the Atlantic Coast Conference, but there were some good players on this team—big, strong guys, in some cases three or four years older than me. Guys like Kevin Roberson of Vermont, who had led the country in blocked shots. Less than a year after graduating, Kevin was killed by a drunk driver in his hometown of Buffalo, and I think most people have forgotten just how good a player he was. But, man, he kicked my ass all over the floor in practice. So did the coaches, Jack and Karl Fogel of Northeastern, another fast-talking tough guy. They were on me from the jump, especially Coach Phelan. I was his whipping boy in the pretournament practices, and even after we got overseas. I'd come back to my room after getting humiliated and berated in front of the whole team, and I'd wonder why I'd even been invited. I also questioned Jack's motivational techniques.

You're going to go at me in front of all these guys, when you know I have to play against them next year?

He sure did. I came back to my room one night seething with anger, looking for a little compassion from my roommate, Ron Moore, who was also my teammate at Hartford. Ron was older than me, tougher, and at the time a much better basketball player. He'd also been through the wars with Coach Phelan, and along the way had earned Jack's trust and respect.

"I can't believe the way Coach is treating me," I whined.

Ron just laughed. "No, man, you don't get it. You've got to be stronger."

He was right. And Jack was right (although I still don't necessarily agree with his tactics).

I stopped feeling sorry for myself and decided to outwork everyone—not just in games, but in practice as well. When Coach Phelan yelled at me, which he continued to do, I feigned indifference. Inside, the anger remained, but I channeled it properly. I wanted to prove to Jack, and to anyone else who may have been watching, that I was neither weak nor overmatched. I was one of the first to arrive for practice each day, and one of the last to leave. In games, I played with a chip on my shoulder. I embraced the idea that you get out of life (and sports) exactly what you put into it. It was such a simple formula, but it worked.

By the end of the trip Ron was the leading scorer on the team, and I was the second-leading scorer. I remember standing outside a club one night, talking to a girl from Finland, trying to communicate and make a connection despite the fact that she spoke almost no English. Coach Fogel walked by, did a double take, and stopped. As he looked at the girl, he pointed at me.

"NBA," he said. And then again, slower. "N–B–A!"

The girl smiled. I just kind of threw my hands in the air. Coach Fogel laughed and walked away. I figured he was trying to help me with a hookup. Turns out he was making an honest prediction.

THINGS HAPPENED PRETTY QUICKLY after that trip. I moved into the starting lineup, averaged 19.7 points and 10.4 rebounds per game as a sophomore, and was named first-team all-NAC. As a junior I took another jump: 27.6 points, 9.9 rebounds, and 3.7 blocks. Our team was awful—we won only six games—but I was the second-leading scorer in the country. That's kind of the way it went for me throughout my college career.

Somehow, through a combination of effort, luck, coaching, and timing, I became one of the best players in the country. But basketball is a team game—maybe the ultimate team game—and Hartford was still a fledgling program. Unless you're LeBron James, capable of going off for 50 or 60 points, you can't win games by yourself. I wasn't that kind of player. Opponents knew that even if I scored 30 points and had 10 or 15 rebounds, it usually wouldn't be enough. I tried to be a good teammate and not let the frustration show, but for the most part I had to be content with focusing on my own development. The final score just wasn't much of a factor.

At the beginning of my senior year, *Sports Illustrated* did a story on me with the headline "America's Best-Kept Secret." For the photo shoot on campus, the University of Hartford wanted to have some other student-athletes around me in the stands. I was actually embarrassed by the attention: *You're going to get students out of class for me? Come on . . .* By this point I knew I'd have a chance to play in the NBA, but I didn't know where I stood in the pecking order. I was at Hartford, not Michigan. Other guys who figured to be drafted high that year were household names: Chris Webber, Jalen Rose, Bobby Hurley, Calbert Cheaney. Great players. Blue-chip recruits out of high school, college all-Americans. Stats notwithstanding, I was a nobody by comparison. Whenever I had a chance to play against better competition, I did just fine. But it wasn't like there were agents swarming all around me.

Later I heard that the Celtics were ready to take me in the top twenty of the draft after my junior year, but somehow the message—or at least the sincerity of the message—never got through. That was probably a good thing. I had played well at some camps in the summer before my senior year, and considered the possibility of entering the draft, but the truth is, I was terrified by the prospect of leaving school. It wasn't just that I had doubts about whether I could handle the level of competition in the NBA, I also questioned my own maturity, and I feared the great unknown. I wasn't much of a partier at all in college—didn't start going out until my junior year, even then only once a week or so, and didn't drink very much. I was hopelessly inexperienced with women as well—didn't lose my virginity until I got to college, and even then I was more of a steady-girlfriend type than a player.

So I liked the University of Hartford. I was comfortable and happy. I was close to home. At the time, I couldn't imagine giving all that up to take a shot at playing in the pros. Sure, it was flattering to know that people in the NBA were looking at me seriously, but I was more concerned about how I would tell my parents that I was dropping out of school to play professional basketball. And if you're not confident and mature enough to tell your parents you're leaving school to play in the NBA (for millions of dollars), then you're probably not ready for the job.

Instead, I stayed in school, got my degree, and continued to grow and improve. I averaged 28.3 points per game as a senior (fourth best in the country), finished as Hartford's all-time leading scorer, and wound up being taken eighth by the Milwaukee Bucks in the first round of the 1993 NBA draft. In every way imaginable, especially from an economic standpoint, it was a life-altering development. Today, thanks to salary caps and the collective bargaining agreement, rookie contracts in the NBA are strictly regulated: a maximum of two years, with a team option on years three and four, and a ceiling that prevents anyone from backing up the Brinks truck right out of college. But in 1993, you got what you could get, as quickly as you could get it. My first contract was for ten years and a total of $18 million. Most of the guys around me in the draft thought that was crazy. Six years was more common, with a couple of players opting for eight. The negotiating of professional sports contracts has always been a risky proposition, for both players and management. The player wants long-term security, of course, but if he signs for ten years, as I did, and he becomes an all-star in year three, with significantly greater market value . . . well, management naturally would prefer not to renegotiate that deal. My agents made sure that I had an option to leave after the third year, but I didn't care. I was looking at $1.8 million a year: more money than I had ever dreamed of earning.

My parents were shocked. In fact, it wasn't until the night of the draft that they truly came to believe that I could make a living playing in the NBA. And a good living at that. I don't mean to sound like they were unsupportive; they weren't. But they were far from helicopter parents. I didn't have a soccer mom or a dad who coached biddy ball. My parents were not invested in my athletic career, they were merely casual observers. Early in my college career they didn't attend many games, and even when I was a senior and they were fixtures courtside, smiling proudly and enjoying themselves as loyal Hartford fans, I don't think they understood what they were seeing. When I would talk about playing professional ball, they would express quiet skepticism, as if to say, *Can you really make a living doing that? Playing a game?*

Their ambivalence was understandable. My father was a mechanic and a preacher. Mom worked an office job. They did hard, honest, tangible work, and on Friday afternoon they would pick up a paycheck and deposit it in the bank. They knew and trusted a hands-on employment experience.

If someone asked my father, "What do you do for a living?" he could say, "I fix cars." Very straightforward and easily understood. So all this stuff about the pros . . . it was foreign to my parents; it was fantasy. What they knew of the NBA consisted mainly, if not exclusively, of guys like Michael Jordan and others near his level. You were either a superstar or a bust, a multimillionaire or a guy playing for meal money. They had no idea that everyone in the NBA was a tremendous athlete being very well compensated for his services. And they certainly didn't think I had an opportunity to be one of the elite members of an already elite fraternity.

For all of us, though, it became reality on that June night in 1993, at Joe Louis Arena in Detroit. For my parents, especially, I think it all started to make sense when they entered the building and got a strong whiff of success. This was a big deal, and their son was part of it.

As expected, Chris Webber, the gifted power forward from Michigan's Fab Five, was the first pick overall, selected by the Orlando Magic. BYU freshman Shawn Bradley, a seven-foot-six center, was the second pick, for the Philadelphia 76ers, followed by Penny Hardaway of the University of Memphis (Golden State Warriors), Jamal Mashburn of Kentucky (Dallas Mavericks), Isaiah Rider of UNLV (Minnesota Timberwolves), Calbert Cheaney of Indiana (Washington Bullets), and the point guard Bobby Hurley of Duke (Sacramento Kings).

That brought us to the eighth pick, which belonged to the Milwaukee Bucks.

Here's the thing about the draft: If you're among the top players—let's say, the first five to ten—you usually know ahead of time where you are likely to land. There is too much at stake for teams to leave much to chance. If a team is seriously interested in a prospect, that player is brought in for extensive interviews and usually a serious workout. By the time a coach and general manager settle on a draft pick, they have done their due diligence and are as confident as possible that the player will fill a need for many years to come. Unless of course the goal is simply to acquire that player and trade him for someone else whom the team really needs. But it goes without saying that when your business model (and your job) is predicated on predicting the reliability and potential of young men barely out of their teens . . . mistakes can be made.

As they said in *Sports Illustrated*, I was college basketball's best-kept secret, but by the time the draft rolled around, everyone in the NBA knew who I was and had determined whether my small-school stardom would translate to professional achievement. Like every other potential high first-round draft pick, I had been poked and prodded, quizzed and questioned. Ordinarily, mid-major players (those not from the power conferences) will play in several senior showcases at the end of the season. These are typically a way for small-college players to get exposure to scouts who may have overlooked them during the season. My agents, however, steered me away from the postseason showcases, their theory being that I was a lottery pick, not a kid just hoping to hit the board sometime in the late first round; and lottery picks did not play in these events. They ended up being right, but in retrospect I'm pretty sure that their decision was based primarily on inexperience.

My agents were Walter Luckett and Lou Albanese. Walter was a legendary baller out of Kolbe High School in Bridgeport, Connecticut. The guy graduated in the early 1970s and fifty years later was still the all-time New England career prep scoring leader. He averaged a triple-double in his senior year and was named national high school player of the year; in his freshman year at Ohio University, he was featured on the cover of *Sports Illustrated*. Although he played briefly in the NBA, a knee injury shortened Walter's career, and he eventually returned to Connecticut and built a successful business career.

My connection to Walter? He had gotten to know my mother through work. Walter would occasionally talk to Mom about me and how I was doing. Eventually he and a business associate, Lou Albanese, an investment broker from Westport, offered to help with the management of my basketball career. In the beginning their plan was to simply introduce me to the proper parties—which they did, including Bob Woolf, who was one of the top sports agents in the field at the time. In the end, though, Walter and Lou decided they could handle the job themselves, which was fine by me. They were exactly what I needed, a couple of guys with only one client, and a connection to my family. I wasn't ready for Bob Woolf or David Falk or anyone else of that magnitude. And I loved the fact that they were so excited to be representing me; I could see it on their faces.

Lou and Walt decided that in the months leading up to the draft, my time would be better served by working out for individual teams, rather than participating in showcase events designed for players who weren't even assured of being drafted, let alone being potential lottery picks. So they arranged several workouts and interviews, in the hope of generating even more buzz. A good individual workout can do that, as GMs and coaches tend to share information. A bad one, of course, can kill you, as can a poor interview performance. I didn't know much about the whole process, but I had faith in Walt and Lou, and in my own ability.

Some people thought we were making a huge mistake. Chief among those was Marty Blake, who at the time was the NBA's director of scouting.

"This is ridiculous," Marty told me. "You need to go to these tournaments and show that you can play."

But I believed in my agents, and in the path we had chosen. Marty was one of the most respected evaluators of talent the NBA had ever known. He knew the game, both on and off the court, and I'm sure he felt like he was giving me sound advice. But I was willing to gamble that my agents were right.

"You know what, Marty?" I said. "I think I'm comfortable."

The only problem was, I may have been a little *too* comfortable. You see, I didn't really understand the intricacies of the entire process of working out and interviewing with individual teams. Today the top college prospects are well versed in the proceedings. They are trained not only for the rigors of a physical test, but they also practice interview techniques. The idea is to demonstrate exceptional athletic prowess and fitness on the floor, and maturity and intellect off the floor. A strong workout will convince coaches and front office personnel that an athlete represents a solid investment over the long term.

Unfortunately, I hadn't played much basketball since the end of my senior season. I was training lightly, staying in decent shape, but I wasn't nearly as fit as I'd been a few months earlier. Truth is, we all greatly underestimated the possibility that some of these workouts would be extremely arduous. I figured they would be nothing more than a glorified physical examination and a shootaround. In some cases, that was true. In others . . . well, not so much.

The Warriors brought me in for a workout and interview, but I knew ahead of time that they weren't very serious about drafting me. Golden State had the third pick, and while we had heard rumors that I would go in the top ten, no one had speculated that I might go as high as the top three. Indeed, the interview was brief and perfunctory, and the workout— just me and one of the assistant coaches—was fairly low key. I did nothing to hurt or help my stock, and left that session knowing only that I wouldn't be playing for Golden State and coach Don Nelson the next year.

More intense, though, were my workouts with the Detroit Pistons, Denver Nuggets, and Milwaukee Bucks. These were teams that had expressed legitimate interest in me, and the workouts and interviews reflected the seriousness of their intent. Detroit was kind of a disaster—I was totally gassed within the first five to ten minutes. Same thing in Milwaukee, just brutal. Two hours of intense drills and cardio work with virtually no rest. Take two dribbles, dunk, do it again. Over and over, until your shoulders ache and your lungs are burning. Then a dozen or more suicides. Then shooting drills, agility tests, one-on-one competitions, all designed to measure and assess not just skill and athleticism, but also endurance, commitment, and desire.

I nearly quit halfway through because I thought I was going to pass out or vomit. Not exactly the best way to impress the coach, Mike Dunleavy, especially when he was doing the workout right alongside me! Mike was a former NBA player, and he was still in great shape, as feisty and tough as ever, but let's be honest: he was also nearly forty years old.

I was twenty-two and supposedly a potential lottery pick; I couldn't afford to get beaten up or outplayed by my future coach. Not a good look. So I choked back the nausea and pushed through the workout. Afterward, Coach Dunleavy told me I did well, but I wasn't so sure.

The Denver Nuggets actually put me through the most comprehensive screening: two days of interviews and workouts. Being an East Coast guy who had spent his entire life at sea level, I felt the altitude in Denver almost as soon as the plane touched down, and I worried that it was going to have an impact on my performance. By this time, though, I had worked out for a few teams and knew what to expect. I'd also been in the gym often enough to have regained a good measure of fitness. The Nuggets put me through a series of tests and workouts, all of which I handled pretty easily. I knew I was doing well. Then I met with the staff and answered their questions in exactly the right manner. I knew there was a script to the proceedings, and I followed it to the letter:

> QUESTION: *Son, what do you think you need to do in order to play in the NBA?*
> ANSWER: *I need to keep working hard, sir. I'm going to continue to train, and get stronger and improve every facet of my game.*

However, I was not prepared for the question that I was asked by coach and general manager Bernie Bickerstaff near the end of the interview.

"Well, what are we going to do, Vin?"

"Sir?"

Bernie smiled. "What are we going to do about you?"

Such a vague and open-ended query; it almost seemed like he was trying to trip me up.

"I'm not sure I understand, Mr. Bickerstaff. Like I said, I'll work hard and get ready for the draft, and . . ."

He held up a hand, shook his head.

"That's not what I mean. I know you can play in the league, and I'd like you to play for the Nuggets. But how can we make that happen?"

Suddenly I realized what was happening. Our conversation had moved from one of assessment to one of strategy.

"Here's what I'm talking about," Bernie said. "We have to figure out a way to make sure you're still around at number nine, when we pick." He paused, looked around the room. Everyone was kind of smiling and nodding.

"Okay," I said, playing along.

Bernie leaned forward in his chair, as if he were about to say something secretive.

"Over the next couple days you may hear some things about yourself that you're not going to like."

At first I was confused. Who would say anything bad about me?

"I'm sorry, Mr. Bickerstaff. I don't understand."

He smiled. "Well, you might hear that your workout didn't go so well. But don't pay any attention to it, okay? It's just talk."

Finally, the lightbulb went on. The Nuggets were prepared to float rumors about my performance—or, rather, my supposed subpar performance—in an effort to reduce interest in me on draft day. I was naive enough to be surprised by this sort of tactic. Did teams really lie about a prospect's performance? Apparently they did. Or maybe "lie" is too strong a

word. It was more a matter of underselling to keep competing bidders away. Just business, I guess.

Except it didn't work.

Looking back on it, the most awesome part of my draft
experience was the mystery of it all. I was so inexperienced
and utterly lacking in guile that I was perfectly content to
simply be there. I'm pretty sure that everyone who was
drafted ahead of me knew exactly when their name would
be called, and who would do the calling. I honestly did not
know. So I sat there with my little entourage—my mother
and father, and three of my Hartford teammates, Mike Bond,
Marlon Toon, and Paul Spence—and soaked it all in. It wasn't
so much that I was nervous; I was just excited to be there,
and to be a part of it. I watched the parade of major college
players drafted ahead of me—guys from Michigan and Duke,
from UNLV and Kentucky—and I still found it almost in-
comprehensible that I was sitting there in the same room
with them. But I was, and the fact that I belonged there was
driven home when NBA commissioner David Stern walked
to the podium and announced my name.

"With the eighth pick in the 1993 NBA draft, the Milwaukee Bucks select . . . Vin Baker from the University of
Hartford!"

Despite knowing that this moment was coming at some
point in the evening, I was still shocked. I didn't even stand
up right way. It actually took a few seconds for the words to
penetrate my brain.

Oh . . . hey . . . that's me!

I felt like a little kid on Christmas morning, thrilled at the
wonder of it all, at the sheer magic of the moment. I tried to
maintain my composure, but I was so pumped up. It was all
I could do to keep from sprinting to the stage and hugging

Mr. Stern. But I kept it under control. I kissed my mom, embraced my dad, thanked my friends, and slowly made my way to the front of the room, smiling so hard that I thought I might cry.

And I remember thinking, *How can life ever get any better than this?*

3

★ ★ ★

THE ROOKIE

My rookie year was a bit of a roller-coaster ride. I was so nervous and concerned about my fitness that on the first day of training camp I went for a jog around the city. I got about five blocks from the hotel before realizing how foolish I must have looked.

Go back to your room, you idiot. This isn't going to help.

Milwaukee is a small market and I was a comparatively unknown commodity, so I had to kind of grow into my stardom there. It wasn't given to me as it was to some of the other guys in the draft. A few of my teammates, and not a small percentage of fans, had hoped that the Bucks would have drafted a more recognizable name who would immediately bring some attention to the franchise and sell tickets. I wasn't that guy, so my assimilation was a bit funky. Nothing was handed to me. As was the case at Hartford, the coaching staff and front office viewed me as a project that would take time to develop. But I was competitive and set goals for myself.

The first three months, I came off the bench. Mike Dunleavy was a generally patient coach and a good teacher, but I bristled under the restraint. When I looked around the league, I noticed that every other player who had been drafted in the top ten was either starting or getting big minutes. But not me. Mike brought me along slowly on a team that frankly wasn't very good, and I did not handle the process well. I'd get into the game, play six or seven minutes, get pulled out, and as I walked to the end of the bench, I'd feel the emotion rising in my throat.

"Why the fuck did you pick me if you don't think I can play?" I'd grumble to Mike. More often than not, he would just ignore me. And then, after the game, we'd talk. I know I was wrong in how I handled things. As humble as I was, I still wanted to play, and I couldn't control my emotions. They were paying me a lot of money and I thought I could do things to help the team. But Mike couldn't see it in me.

There were other forces at work, as well. Midway through the season—a really bad season for the Bucks, I might add—we traveled to New Jersey for a game against the Nets. Since it was an East Coast game, not too far from my hometown, a lot of my friends and relatives and former teammates were in attendance. And I did not play one second. Sat on the bench the entire game. I was healthy, fit, and certainly capable of contributing . . . something. But there it was in the box score: "DNP (coach's decision)." I wasn't the best player in the league, or even the best rookie, but I sure as hell was good enough to get a few minutes for a struggling

Milwaukee Bucks team, especially when you consider that I was a first-round draft pick who was supposed to be part of the team's foundation for the future. But as the game went on, and I continued to sit on the bench, growing angrier by the minute, I began to suspect that maybe I was sitting precisely for that reason: because I could help us win.

And we weren't trying to win.

This is a dirty secret in the NBA (although not such a secret anymore). As the season drags on and the playoffs spin out of reach, teams do not always give their best effort. At that point, positioning for the upcoming draft becomes more important than positioning in the current standings. And the worse your record, the more likely you are to have a high draft pick the following year. I'm not suggesting that players go in the tank. Sure, it becomes tough to stay motivated late in the year when you're losing a lot and you don't have a shot at the playoffs. But most guys in the NBA are ferociously competitive; they hate to lose, and so they give their best effort every night. Injuries, travel, fatigue—all of these can affect a player's performance and a game's outcome. Of even greater impact, though, are the decisions made by coaches and front office personnel. The moves can be obvious—trade or release a player who might actually be capable of helping you win, bench a guy who should be on the floor—or subtle, such as simply neglecting to make roster changes that would improve your chances of winning. Either way, the outcome is the same: more losses, fewer victories.

As I sat that night in New Jersey, my butt glued to the bench, I became convinced that we were not doing everything we could to win the game, or most games, in fact. My playing time was a casualty of that strategy. By the time the game ended, I was furious. We walked into the locker room and immediately I confronted Coach Dunleavy. Probably not the smartest thing for a rookie to do.

"Mike, that's bullshit that you didn't play me tonight, and you know it."

He was a few feet ahead of me as I yelled, and he instantly turned to face me.

"You're out of line, Vin." Before I could say another word, one of my teammates jumped in between us and basically tackled me—a completely unnecessary act, since I had no intention of getting into a physical altercation with my coach. I just wanted to let him know that I was angry, and that I knew something was up. But the intervention only escalated matters. It turned a verbal dispute into something that appeared to be much more serious. I tried to steady myself, and as I regained my footing, Mike shouted out across the locker room.

"Let him go! Let that motherfucker go!"

This was the interesting thing about Mike. He knew basketball. The guy was a good player and a good coach. He also was something of a chameleon—slick businessman one moment, thoughtful mentor the next moment, and hard-ass New Yorker the next. Right now, in the locker room? This was New York Mike. He wasn't going to get called out by a player, especially a rookie. Didn't matter that he was eight inches shorter than me, sixty pounds lighter, and almost two decades older. I had challenged his integrity, his leadership, his manhood. Can't say I really blame him for getting upset. I just think he overreacted a little. But stuff happens in the locker room. It comes with the territory.

Mike knew which buttons to push with me, and he tried just about all of them. I remember a game in Seattle shortly after the All-Star Break. I was starting to play a little more, but I had a tendency to overthink things. I would analyze and question and envision scenarios that would or would not work. Again, this was a product of the anxiety that had been an issue for me since I was a little kid. I was afraid of making mistakes, screwing up, and getting called out by the coaches and publicly humiliated. I figured the better prepared I was, the less likely that was to happen. But basketball, like most athletic endeavors, is as much about improvisation as it is preparation. You spend too much time in your head, and you're bound to screw up.

At halftime I asked Mike a question. I don't even remember the nature of the question, but it clearly caused him to bristle. Seattle's top rookie that year was Ervin Johnson, a six-foot-eleven center out of the University of New Orleans. Johnson was the twenty-third pick in the draft, so he barely made it into the first round, a point Coach Dunleavy decided to drive home at precisely that moment. I had barely finished my question when Mike began shaking his head, as a look that can best be described as disgust came across his face.

"Vin, can I just tell you something right now?"

"Sure, Coach."

"All that shit means nothing. All these questions, all the stuff you're worried about and thinking about—it's absolutely meaningless."

"But, Coach, I was just wondering—"

He raised a hand, moved closer to my face. "Stop. Please. Just stop! Right now Ervin Johnson is in that locker room, and he knows he kicked your ass in the first half. You know what he's saying to himself?"

Actually, I hadn't even thought about it, so Mike enlightened me.

"He's saying, 'How in the hell was that motherfucker the

eighth pick, and I was only the twenty-third?' That's what he's saying about you right now. And you're asking me stupid questions? Just play ball."

Then he walked away. Never did answer my question. But you know what? The tactic worked. I played better in the second half of that game, and throughout the second half of the season. In a way, Mike took a blueprint from Jack Phelan. He wasn't going to coddle me or try to make me feel good when I wasn't playing up to my potential, and he wasn't going to back down when I behaved petulantly. Instead, he constantly challenged me to play harder and more aggressively, and if I didn't, he would let me know it. After a while I found a way to channel the anger that resulted from these sparring sessions. Instead of feeling like I wanted to grab Mike by the throat, I would take out my frustration on my opponent. This, of course, was exactly what Coach Dunleavy wanted to see. It was like he was trying to unleash the Incredible Hulk that was hiding somewhere in my massive but timid frame.

"You know what people in the league say about you?" Mike said to me one day after practice?"

"What's that, Coach?"

"That you're a nice guy. You're a good guy. And that's fine, Vin—most of the time. But they know that when you're pissed off, you'll bring it. So you know what their attitude is? 'Let's just not say anything to him, and let's just keep him nice.' That's why you don't hear much trash-talking. It's not because they like you, although they probably do. It's because they don't want to make you mad; they want you soft and happy. You're easy to beat that way."

I didn't know what to think. The notion of being a nice, friendly, polite person had always appealed to me. It was my nature. I didn't like confrontation. I didn't like the loss of control that came with angry outbursts. That's why I'd cry when I got yelled at: because I was swallowing all the hurt and anger.

"So here's what we've gotta do," Mike continued. "We have to find a way to bring that out in you." He paused. "How do we do that, Vin? How do we get you pissed off every single game?"

The answer came in the form of a steady torrent of disappointment and disrespect. That year the NBA held its first rookie game during All-Star weekend in Minneapolis. A Midwestern venue not far from my NBA home, and I wasn't even a part of it. The top twenty players, subjectively speaking, were invited to participate in the rookie game. I had been the eighth pick in the draft, and I was not invited. That was an embarrassment; it also was appropriate given my modest output. Granted, some of this was beyond my control: you need playing time to show what you'e capable of doing. But that's a tricky thing in any sport. Once you are in the doghouse, it can be nearly impossible to find an exit. You have to make the most of every minute, prove yourself worthy in both games and practice, and somehow maintain a positive and professional attitude. To varying degrees, I failed at all these things in the first half of my rookie year.

Eventually I stopped whining and did exactly what Coach Dunleavy had suggested. Instead of choking back the disappointment and anger—instead of feeling sorry for myself—I used it to fuel my performance on the basketball court. And it worked! My minutes slowly increased after the All-Star Break. Pretty soon I was in the starting lineup. At the end of the 1993–94 season I was named to the NBA All-Rookie first team. Averaged 13.5 points and 7.6 rebounds—very respectable numbers for a rookie, particularly one who wasn't playing all that much early in the year. In just a few months I went from not even being among the top twenty rookies—damn near a bust—to being in the top five. I felt vindicated. I felt . . . happy.

In hindsight, I can see that Coach Dunleavy was 100 percent right. He knew I wasn't ready for the NBA when I first got to Milwaukee. I had to develop that energy, that motivation. I had to get hungry. Everyone gets knocked around in life; the trick is figuring out how to bounce back from the beating.

4

★ ★ ★

"HOW BAD CAN IT BE?"

t's interesting. People who abuse alcohol are known as al-
coholics. People who abuse all manner of pharmaceutical
products and other illicit substances are generally lumped
under the pejorative heading of "drug addict." But marijuana users mostly get a pass. The names for the person
who smokes weed all day, every day—"stoner," "pothead,"
whatever—are fairly benign. They lack the sting of accusation and weakness—of recklessness and damage—associated
with labeling someone an alcoholic or a drug addict. And,
yeah, maybe it's not quite as bad, but I'm telling you right
now—weed is at the very least psychologically addictive,
and it can and will screw up your life. It also happens to be
a serious problem within professional sports in general, and

the NBA in particular. How bad? I'd say, on average, five or six players on every team are smoking weed on a regular basis—and by "regular," I mean, every day. Including game days.

I didn't smoke at all—not once—until I got to the pros. In my rookie year I was a young man with a growing degree of fame, a substantial amount of discretionary income, and sudden access to a variety of mood-altering substances. I was a young man who discovered almost by accident that the sometimes crippling anxiety and shyness he faced as a teenager were greatly mitigated by a few drinks or a couple of hits of weed, and whose young body—the body of a highly trained professional athlete—seemed more than capable of withstanding the occasional late night on the town. That's the insidious nature of addiction: you don't see it coming until it's too late, until all the fun is drained of the experience and you're left with nothing but anguish and loneliness and regret.

It doesn't happen overnight.

For all intents and purposes I was a grown man when I arrived in Milwaukee for my rookie season with the Bucks. Chronologically, legally, physically, I was an adult, supposedly capable of caring for myself and making decisions that would enhance my career, rather than detract from it. Practically speaking, though, I was still an adolescent (and keep in mind, I was twenty-two years old; I can't imagine what it must be like today, when so many of the top draft picks are coming out after only one year of college, many still in their teens—what a nightmare for both the player and his new employer). Like a lot of rookies, I enlisted the services of a couple of friends on this journey. Got a nice place to live, one with more space than I'd ever need, and invited them to join me. Here was the agreement: I would pick up their living expenses, and they would pick up . . . well, nothing. Basically, I was paying for companionship and support. I didn't look at it that way at the time, and I know it sounds crass and cold, but essentially that's the way it worked. I was afraid of being alone in a new town. I wanted to see familiar faces when I came home from practice or games. I wanted that same feeling I had in college, when you walk down the hallway of your dorm and just about every door is open, and you can count on a friendly conversation at any time of the day or night, when you never have to worry about finding someone with whom to have lunch or dinner.

Merely filling the day proved to be something of a challenge. I know some people scoff at the very concept of the "student-athlete" in big-time college sports, but for those who play at the mid-major level, and who spend four years on campus, honestly and diligently working toward a degree (I put myself in that category), it's an appropriate term. At Hartford I had very little downtime. Between classes, study hall, homework, practice, meals, games, meetings, travel, and film sessions, I sometimes felt as if there weren't enough hours in the day. I very quickly discovered that the NBA is a job, and a serious and demanding one at that, but it isn't a 24/7 experience, the way it is when you are a college athlete. You find yourself coming home at noon after a morning shoot-around or practice, and suddenly you're looking at four or five hours with nothing to do. I understand now how it's supposed to work—how the great ones take care of themselves and fill that empty time with endeavors that can further their careers—or with healthy interaction with friends and family. Me? I just wanted to make sure I wasn't sad and homesick.

Because I was somewhat shy and reserved, I made new

friends slowly and tentatively, but eventually I connected with a few guys on the Bucks—Eric Murdock, Todd Day, and Frank Brickowski—and through them I was introduced to the time-honored practice of burning the candle at both ends. I want to make one thing clear: when I was with the Bucks, the great majority of my partying occurred on the road. This is partly attributable to the fact that Milwaukee is kind of a sleepy town (by major metro standards); there aren't a ton of late-night options, and if you screw up and behave inappropriately, news of that behavior is likely to find its way back to your coach or GM or the local media and fans. And let's be honest: Married guys stay home when they're home. On the road, many of them go out and act like they aren't married (or otherwise attached). Just the way it is.

It began casually enough: most nights on the road, after a game, we'd hit a club (and by club, I mean strip club—most of the time, anyway), where we'd drink hard and fast, drop hundreds if not thousands of dollars, and then go back to the hotel and sleep it off—sometimes with female companionship, sometimes not. Either way, it was fun. I need to be perfectly blunt about that: in the beginning, at least, the late nights were a blast. I liked going out after games; I liked walking into a club wearing an expensive suit, looking like a ballplayer out on the town, a guy prepared to make it rain. I wanted everyone to know that I wasn't some chump—I was young and successful, so why not enjoy the fruits of my labor? Of course, that's shallow and stupid, but it's also part of growing up. Most young guys go through some version of this and come out on the other side no worse for wear. I figured I had it all under control. And I did, in the early days, anyway. I had no idea of the demons lurking within me, of the propensity for alcoholism and addiction. I just knew that drinking made me feel good—that warm rush that came with the first shot, and the subsequent eroding of inhibitions. Whenever I drank—and it wasn't all that often in my rookie year—I became funnier. All my life I had been the kind of guy who would stand pinned to a wall in a crowded room, afraid to talk with people, afraid to be seen or heard or judged. Now I'd go out after a game, have a few drinks, and suddenly I'd be dancing like a fool! An inebriated, completely uninhibited, fun-loving fool.

Everything changed when I drank. Typically tongue-tied around women, I would morph into a smooth-talking pickup artist. Not just friendly, but almost aggressive. I was a star athlete in college, but if a woman wanted to meet me, she had to make the first move. I wasn't going to risk getting rejected. But I'd watch some of the guys on the Bucks and the way they acted when we were out, totally in control, drawing in women like a magnet, and I'd think: *Yeah, that's the way I want to be. I want to talk like a pro athlete, not like some kid who's harboring his Baptist ministry in his stomach. I don't want to be the preacher's son anymore.*

Slowly but surely, I lost my faith; I turned my back on the core values I'd been taught. I became a different person—and alcohol fueled that transformation.

I'd never been to a strip club before I got to college, and maybe only a couple of times before I got to the NBA. But I became indoctrinated pretty quickly. Professional athletes like strip clubs—high-end strip clubs—not merely because they are filled with attractive, naked women, but because they offer a degree of privacy and discretion you won't find in a regular club. If you're a rich and famous athlete interested in having a few drinks and hooking up with a young lady, the last place you want to go is a regular club or bar. First of all—and this is especially true today, in an era of omnipresent social media, when every cell phone is a camera and every patron a link to TMZ—your every move is likely to be documented. You don't want to be at a club, working the whole "What's your name? What's your sign?" thing in front of an audience. Very few guys are looking for a new wife or girlfriend when they venture out on the road after a game. They are looking for a good time, with no strings attached. Simple as that. When you go to a strip club, everyone understands the parameters of the evening. The club owner tries to provide a degree of privacy to his high-rolling customers. The customer agrees to throw around a lot of cash and to behave in a manner that won't cause trouble. And the dancer agrees to show the customer considerable attention—attention that might carry over to a point well beyond the end of the show. It's not exactly prostitution. It's more of an understanding:

I've got all the money you possibly could want, and you've got exactly what I need.

There were some strip clubs that crossed certain lines of protocol and decorum—not to mention legality—by offering private rooms in which sexual activity would occasionally take place. For the most part, though, the club was merely a place for the athlete to meet a potential partner for the night. To drink and party with his buddies while showering the dancers with far more money and tips than they would ever make during a normal shift.

In return . . . well, that was left up to the patron and the dancer. If they struck up a conversation, and decided at some point that they wanted to leave together and return to the athlete's hotel room, so be it. Two consenting adults are allowed to have sex, right? Is this prostitution, or something more subtle? I know that I never thought of the strippers in this manner, and I don't think they viewed themselves as such. It was more like, "I'll keep the money flowing, and maybe later on you can say thank you."

And when you leave the hotel that night, or very early the next morning, we part ways without anyone feeling hurt or used. It's a professional arrangement based on money and sex and the fulfilling of mutual needs. Nobody gets hurt. Nobody gets pregnant. Nobody tries to trick the other into doing something they don't want to do.

"We just had sex and now I'm leaving. You're okay with that, right?"

"Couldn't be more okay with it. Thank you for the lovely evening."

I know how that sounds—crass and cynical and immoral. It's hard to convey just how normal seemingly deviant behavior can become when you're in the middle of that world. It's a lifestyle, and I got drawn into it. With virtually no experience in these matters, I was at once terrified and fascinated by the strip club culture that seemed to permeate NBA life on the road. I was intimidated by the dancers, worried about spending too much money, fearful that my girlfriend back home would get word of my illicit activities, or that I'd contract a sexually transmitted disease. If you're basically a shy kid who was raised under the hammer of a Baptist minister, even the tamest of strip clubs is going to feel like Caligula's rec room.

That was me. For a while, anyway.

Fortunately (or unfortunately depending on how you look at it), I had an eager and gifted mentor in Frank Brickowski. A decade older than me, with more than a dozen years of professional experience under his belt, Frank was already a basketball lifer by the time I got to Milwaukee. He was six foot ten and 240 well-muscled pounds, so he looked great in a uniform, but he was not the smoothest or the most skilled of players. Frank had been drafted by the Knicks in the third round after graduating from Penn State, and then spent three years kicking around the European leagues before finally catching on with the Seattle SuperSonics. We both came to Milwaukee during the 1993–94 season and he instantly took me under his wing. Although a bit wooden and unglamorous on the basketball court, Frank was impressively smooth around women in virtually any setting. He was the strip club Don of our team, who knew exactly how to make everyone feel comfortable, and how to negotiate the whole deal without a hint of awkwardness or embarrassment.

Believe me, this was an underrated skill, and one we all appreciated.

There were six to eight of us in our drinking group, a mix of black guys and white guys with diverse tastes and interests. Todd Day, for example, liked going to clubs in the 'hood. Jon Barry preferred a more suburban experience. I was basically a follower and did what everyone else wanted to do. Whatever the consensus, Frank could provide the logical venue. Not only did it seem like he had been to every strip club in every NBA city, but he seemed to know most of the dancers by name. And shortly after arriving, he'd have the after-hours party all lined up for everyone who was interested.

Frank got a huge kick out of my youthful exuberance and naïveté. We'd be hanging out in a club somewhere and I'd be talking a mile a minute, throwing back drinks so fast it was scary, my head swiveling as I looked at the girls. Meanwhile, there was Frank, calmly sipping a drink, politely engaging the dancers, behaving like a wily veteran even off the court.

"Vin," he'd say, throwing an arm around my shoulder and laughing. "Settle down. I need you to relax right now."

"Can't do it, Frank. I'm hungry. Know what I mean?"

Frank would nod and laugh reassuringly. "I get it, man. I get it. But you need to find your game here. It's not the fourth quarter yet. Be patient."

He would talk to me that way all the time, even carrying it into the next day's practice. For a guy whose career was built on seriousness and hard work, Frank could be hilarious. Sometimes, after a long night on the town, he'd walk up behind me at the edge of the court, in full view of everyone, and strike up a surreptitious conversation. Frank knew that as a rookie I was nervous about my reputation and how I was viewed by management and the coaching staff. I was the first-round draft pick, the future of the franchise, so even though I would go out once or twice a week, I tried to keep it relatively quiet. To Frank, my reticence was like a scab to pick.

We'd be at practice and Frank would walk over and lean up against me. As I'd stand there listening to Coach Dunleavy, with a serious rookie look on my face, Frank would start whispering.

"You were amazing last night, dude. The way you took that chick down. Seriously impressive."

I'd say nothing, just kind of nod, like we were talking strategy.

"Whoo . . . the body on that girl. You ain't a rookie anymore."

"Knock it off, Frank."

Then he'd laugh quietly, pat me on the back, and walk away.

"You getting all this, Baker?" Coach Dunleavy would say. "Yes, sir."

I can't deny that it was fun. But looking back on it now, after all I've been through, I realize that I was different. There's nothing terribly unusual or scandalous about young men who have money in their pockets living somewhat decadently. Most people learn how to pump the brakes now and then, and eventually they find a slower, safer lane in which to travel. The things that should have served as warning signs, I misinterpreted as subtle gifts: not just the change in personality, but the ability to drink more than everyone else, and to get up the next morning and shake off the effects of a hangover with comparative ease. As an addict in recovery, I now recognize that all these traits were locked into my DNA, just waiting for someone to throw open the door and let them loose. Once enabled, they began the inexorable process of taking ownership of my entire life.

The hangovers I viewed as little more than an annoyance. In the early days, they were rarely debilitating, no matter how late I stayed out or how much I drank. I always bounced back quickly. To be perfectly honest, I often felt weirdly energized by the hangovers. That first sliver of sunlight through the curtains, accompanied by a dull but persistent throbbing above the temple—a headache that announces with great clarity, "Time to pay the toll, my friend!"—would be engaged like an opponent. Later in life the hangovers—too benign a term for what they really are, which is a toxic reaction to alcohol or drugs—would grow worse, and my resolve to fight them would diminish (this is the general trajectory of addiction, incidentally). But in those early years? I was invincible. The morning after always brings two clear choices: buckle down and get on with life, or surrender to the pain.

I did not consider surrender to be a viable option, in part because I didn't want anyone on the coaching staff or in the front office (or even some of my teammates) to know that I had been out late the previous night. So I'd always bring it hard the next day in practice. Indeed, as a rookie, I had some of my best practices, and played some of my best games, after drinking all night and getting just a few hours of sleep.

I generally went out only once or twice a week in my first year, but when I did go out, I drank with purpose. We all did, and that purpose was to get drunk. I had just left college, so basketball—and all that it had given me—was still something I considered sacred. At first I worried that the late nights might have a negative effect, so I tried not to go out too often. But the more I saw of the NBA, the more I came to realize that drinking was the norm, and abstaining was unusual. It was a lifestyle: the freedom, the money, the women, the drugs, the alcohol. They were all part of the plan. You could say no, of course, but it didn't seem like many people did that. And the decision to go out or to remain in the hotel after a game had absolutely nothing to do with how the team played that night. You could win or lose, you could score 30 points or never get off the bench. Didn't matter. After the game you were going to shower, get something to eat, and hit a club. At first I was surprised at the way guys would shake off a loss or a bad performance. Soon, though, I got the message:

This is the NBA, bro. This is what we do.

You know what else "we" do in the NBA, bro? We smoke weed. Lots of it.

I can recall with some clarity (considering how inebriated I was) the first time I smoked marijuana. It was New Year's Day (or night, actually), and I was hanging out with my college roommate and a few other guys at Todd Day's house. After several hours of steady holiday drinking while watching football games, I reached the saturation point. This is a hard thing to explain. I was twenty-two years old and had never taken so much as a single hit of weed, hadn't really even been tempted. I had grown up believing not only that smoking marijuana was bad for you—bad for the brain, bad for the lungs, bad for the heart—but also that it invited all kinds of trouble beyond the merely physical. It was, after all, still illegal, and I was the kind of kid who was terrified of getting in trouble, incurring the wrath of his parents, and generally letting people down. So I abstained. By the time I was a senior at Hartford, it was almost a running joke. My friends and teammates who smoked knew better than to even ask me if I wanted to partake.

In the NBA, however, weed was a much bigger part of the culture; it was everywhere. For the first few months I continued to abstain and nobody really pushed me to change. It was just something guys did, and if you wanted to smoke, there was no shortage of opportunities. We all have free will, and we all are responsible for the choices we make. Repeated exposure to weed, and to guys who smoked weed and seemed to experience no deleterious effects, eventually had a withering effect.

How bad can it be?

As I sat in the living room at Todd's house, watching one of the guys roll up some weed, I felt a surge of curiosity. I was a little queasy from a day of drinking and overeating, but not quite ready to turn in for the night. I'd been in this position before and had always found it easy to say no thanks when the joint came around. This time, though, I jumped in. I remember glancing over at my college roommate as I took the joint in hand; he wore a look of amusement, if not astonishment. I was such a novice that I didn't even know how to smoke. I took a couple of light hits, didn't inhale too deeply, because I didn't want to gag and make a fool out of myself, and then passed it along. There were no jokes, no words of admonishment. It was no big deal. Except it was. Once lost, virginity cannot be reclaimed. I was no longer a guy who had never smoked weed, had never experimented with drugs in any way. I had crossed that threshold and there was no coming back. Not for me. For me, as it turns out, there are no half measures.

At first I felt nothing, but a short time later, when we went out to a club, it hit me. The combination of alcohol and marijuana left me reeling. I felt like I was floating across the floor. It was the strangest sensation, more psychedelic than the alcohol buzz to which I had grown accustomed. I can't say I liked it, but I didn't find it unpleasant, either. It was just . . . different. As the night wore on, and I resumed drinking, I began to lose control. At one point I went to the bathroom. Inside, just hanging out, were three or four people smoking weed. Random guys I had never met. Ordinarily I would have turned around and walked out. This time, though, with my defenses down, if not completely shattered, I said hello. They seemed friendly enough and quickly offered me a hit. I took it . . . and then took another. And another.

I don't know how much time elapsed, but it must have been a while, because when I got back to our table, Todd asked me if I was okay.

"Yeah, fine, bro. Just smoking some weed in the bathroom."

Todd stared at me quizzically. It was not the response I had anticipated.

"Who you smoking with?" he said.

"I don't know, man. Just some guys."

Todd shook his head, and suddenly I realized that he was pissed. This confused the hell out of me. Todd liked his weed—that was no secret—but he was a year older than me and savvy about his recreational activities. He knew where the line was, and clearly he felt like I had crossed it.

"Don't ever do that again," he said, his tone more parental than collegial.

"What's the big deal?"

He leaned into me. "You're a professional basketball player. You're a rookie. You can't be running around smoking weed with strangers in the bathroom. What the fuck's wrong with you?"

If I hadn't been so drunk, I might have responded angrily to being scolded in this manner. As it was, I didn't really care. I liked Todd and looked up to him. He was a good player; like me, Todd had been drafted eighth overall by the Bucks, so he knew what it was like to be a rookie facing high expectations. Unlike me, he had a reputation for being something of a tough guy both on and off the court, who said what was on his mind, often unfiltered. Todd had grown up in Memphis, played at the University of Arkansas, and felt comfortable in places that were foreign to me. I was drawn to him in a number of ways, so his opinion meant a lot to me.

"Okay, Todd," I said. "I get it. Sorry."

There was another time that season I joined Todd on a trip to Fayetteville, where he was being honored before one of the Arkansas basketball games. We had a road game against the Dallas Mavericks the next night, with a mandatory shootaround in the morning, so the schedule was tight. But the flight from Fayetteville to Dallas was short, so we didn't think it would be a problem.

I was excited about hanging out with Todd at Arkansas. I was his rook and he liked dragging me around, introducing me to people, showing me the ropes. Yet Todd had an edge that could sometimes be off putting. I hadn't felt much of the sting since I'd arrived in Milwaukee, but something weird happened on that trip to Fayetteville. I spent a lot of time at the game meeting Todd's friends and family, teammates and coaches, boosters and alumni. It was all very comfortable and polite and friendly. But after roughly the thirtieth introduction, Todd turned to me and said, "See, that's what I'm saying, man. If you were Alonzo Mourning, I wouldn't have to do all these damn introductions."

I stiffened, waited for him to laugh or poke me in the ribs. Something . . . anything to indicate he was kidding, just busting my balls. But there was nothing. He just sat there and shook his head.

"What's that, Todd?"

He didn't even make eye contact, just kept watching the game. "You know what I'm saying."

I did. I knew exactly what he was saying, and it hurt like hell. By the All-Star Break of my rookie year there were whispers around the league that the Bucks had wasted a high draft pick on a mid-major bust. I hadn't broken out yet, hadn't proved that I deserved the money I was making or the respect of NBA veterans. Todd was only a year ahead of me, and wasn't an all-star himself, but he was the best player on our team and he considered himself to be a straight talker—even when the message was painful. But I also thought he was my friend, and friends didn't dig at each other this way. It was, after all, a little early to be comparing me to Alonzo Mourning, who had for years been one of the best centers in the NBA.

I sat there in stunned silence for a few minutes, waiting for Todd to add something that might soften the blow. But it never came. He was trying to send a message to me. While we may have been friends, Todd seemed to be disappointed in me as a player; if so, that was a painful thing to learn.

That night we went to an apartment and smoked weed with some of Todd's friends. Then we went out to a club, and this time the high hit me hard, probably because there was less alcohol involved. It was a different buzz than what I felt from drinking, more laid-back and relaxed. I liked it. A lot. The night ended with a trip to a local diner, where I experienced a raging case of the munchies. I couldn't stop eating, and I didn't even notice until I was nearly through that the rest of the guys at the table were all staring at me and laughing. For most of the night I had been insisting that the weed hadn't really taken effect. But there was no denying it now.

"You must be feeling something," Todd said, "because you just ate three racks of ribs."

I looked down. My hands were covered with goo. Sauce dripped from my chin. I shrugged and giggled.

"Maybe so."

We missed our flight the next morning, grabbed one that departed a short time later, and went straight to the arena after landing in Dallas. Unfortunately, we still managed to miss the first ten minutes of shootaround, which is not a good idea under the best of circumstances, and certainly ill advised if you are a rookie whose best excuse is that he was out too late the night before. I didn't feel all that hungover, to be honest, but we had screwed up. I'd had a perfect attendance record up to that point, so I didn't know exactly what to expect; my hope was that ten minutes would be deemed a minor transgression and that some leeway would be given considering this was a first offense.

When we arrived the team was gathered at center court in a loose semicircle, with Coach Dunleavy in the middle. Todd and I walked straight to the huddle, acting like we hadn't done anything wrong. Mike saw us coming, stopped talking, and looked straight at Todd.

"You fucking owe me, man. You owe me for this."

He said it with a half smile, so that Todd would get the point but not feel threatened or embarrassed.

"Yeah, man, I know. I got it," Todd said. Then he nodded in my direction. "I'll take Rook's, too."

With that, Coach Dunleavy took a more serious tone. He stared me down for a moment, then cut loose.

"A rookie pulling this shit?" he said, his voice oozing contempt. "Strolling in here late for shootaround? You do know we have a game tonight, right?"

"Yes, sir."

"You got some fucking nerve, son."

My ears were burning by the end of his tirade. I felt small and stupid. That tongue lashing, combined with Todd's comments the previous night, triggered a wave of anxiety that left me wondering whether I even belonged in the league. It's interesting to look back on it now. I began drinking and smoking weed as a way to self-medicate, to try to alleviate some of the insecurity that had long been a problem in my life. But whatever short-term relief I may have experienced, there was always a price to pay. In this particular incident, for example, a night of drinking and smoking weed had caused us to oversleep and show up late for practice. Then again, if I hadn't been out getting high with my boy Todd, I might never have had that moment of clarity: "If you were Alonzo Mourning, I wouldn't have to do all these damn introductions."

Okay, so that's what you think of me? I guess I'll have to change your opinion.

Coach Dunleavy's rant caused me to become more focused. It fueled my desire to become one of the top frontcourt players in the league, and to convince the Bucks and their fans that I was worthy of being the eighth pick in the draft. I cut back on the drinking, went out maybe once a week, or even less in the last couple of months of the season. My play improved dramatically. Weed? I could take it or leave it. And for the most part, I left it.

5

★ ★ ★

PLAYING HIGH

Although I sometimes butted heads with Coach Dunleavy in my rookie year, I also had sympathy for the position he was in. The Bucks were not a good basketball team, and Mike was assigned the task of turning the franchise around. But that doesn't happen overnight. It happens—when it happens—over a period of years, through a combination of good coaching and the acquisition of talent, either through trades or the draft. The goal is always to win as many games as possible, and to perform well in the playoffs; for a select few teams, winning a championship becomes a reasonable goal. Professional basketball is a business, and the teams that win also tend to sell the most tickets and generate the most revenue.

The Milwaukee Bucks were not part of that club.

For any team in a protracted period of rebuilding, challenging decisions must be made. When it becomes apparent that the playoffs are no longer a viable option, management begins to focus less on winning games during the current season and more on creating an atmosphere conducive to winning games at some point in the future. Fans hate to see their team lose, even if it means getting the top pick in the draft—at some point they just stop showing up for games and you wind up with a lot of empty seats and a disgruntled fan base. And players really hate losing. So the burden of managing this chaotic scenario falls on the coach. He tries to keep his team engaged and working hard regardless of the record. He is supposed to develop young talent and placate veterans without winning so often that draft position is compromised. This was the challenge Mike Dunleavy faced in the second half of my rookie season, and I did not envy him one bit.

I felt the weight of this more than most players. Like I said, there were games when I was playing extremely well—games in which we had an opportunity to win—and I'd suddenly be pulled from the lineup. At first I found it confusing—*Are we really trying to lose this game?*—and then it made me angry. Finally, as the losses mounted, resignation set in. A pattern developed. I'd play twenty to thirty minutes, get in a good run, feel good about my performance . . . and then go to the bench. That was player-development time. The end of the game was losing time, and I was often not on the floor. Coach Dunleavy, meanwhile, began handling me differently. He would be softer, more complimentary. Our last trip to New Jersey could not have been more different from the first, when I didn't play at all and got into a shouting match with Mike. It was near the end of the season, and we were all just standing around waiting for a bus to take us from the airport to the hotel, when Mike turned to me and said, loud enough for everyone to hear, "I'm going to grab a cab. Vinnie—let's go."

The vets really let me have it after that. They all started laughing and yelling.

"Uh-oh, he's the franchise now!"

"There he goes—Vin Baker . . . the future of the Bucks."

I'll be honest: it felt good to be viewed this way, and I thought I had earned it. I was one of the top rookies in the league, the leading rebounder on our team, and its third-leading scorer. But there is something undeniably frustrating about being a very good player on a very bad team. And the Bucks were without question a terrible team, compiling a record of 20 wins and 62 losses—at the time, a franchise record for futility; only the Dallas Mavericks (13–69) had a more feeble record.

But there was cause for hope. We had some promising young players and a chance at getting the top pick in the draft. I say "chance," because draft picks are not exactly assigned in reverse order based on the previous year's record. It's a little more convoluted than that, and has been ever since the NBA instituted a draft lottery system in 1985, ostensibly to reduce the likelihood of teams tanking at the end of the regular season to enhance their standing in the draft. Any team that did not make the playoffs went into the lottery, and draft position was based on the outcome of the lottery. So, a team with the league's worst record might wind up with the tenth pick overall, rather than a guaranteed number one.

The lottery system was subsequently modified, but it has

remained basically unchanged over the last quarter century. Any team that does not make the playoffs is automatically entered into the draft lottery, but the system is now weighted: the worse a team's record, the more entries it has in the lottery, thus the greater its chances of receiving a high draft pick. So while incentive to perform badly during the latter stages of the season remains, that incentive is somewhat reduced. Finishing last, after all, does not guarantee the top position in the draft.

In the 1994 draft the Milwaukee Bucks pulled the winning lottery ticket and selected Glenn "Big Dog" Robinson, an explosive six-foot-seven forward out of Purdue University. Glenn was the national college player of the year in 1994. A gifted athlete who could run the floor, shoot, rebound, and play defense, he was deservedly coveted by every team in the NBA. He was considered a legitimate franchise player, a young guy who came with ability and physical attributes tailor-made for the professional game.

I was excited about Glenn's arrival in Milwaukee, because I was confident he could make us a better team. Typical of my mind-set in those days, however, I was also racked by insecurity. A few months earlier I had been the face of the franchise, the "future." Now along comes Big Dog, with a significantly more impressive college résumé than mine. I fretted about my place in the pecking order. I bristled at the club's new marketing campaign, which centered on Glenn. I coveted the attention he received from the national and local media. Most of all, though, I was stung by the way our coaching staff and, especially, my teammates seemed to treat Glenn like he was some sort of savior. All of this, of course, can be distilled down to a simple and not very attractive emotion: jealousy. I was too insecure and immature not to feel threatened by

Glenn. His presence in the lineup was a big deal. Bucks fans had waited a long time for a championship (there has been only one in franchise history, way back in 1971), so it was perfectly understandable that a number one draft pick would provoke some excitement.

I spent way too much time overanalyzing and obsessing about every little thing. It bothered me that Todd Day and Glenn seemed to have an instant connection, which I figured was a big-school thing, Todd having gone to Arkansas and Glenn to Purdue. It annoyed me that some of the other guys on the team—vets who should have known better—were flat-out kissing Glenn's butt. There is a protocol in the NBA, and rookies, no matter how highly touted, are not supposed to be treated deferentially. Then again, maybe I was just upset that I hadn't been afforded the same degree of respect a year earlier. Either way, I had trouble getting past it.

At a preseason press conference, Jon Barry was asked a fairly benign question by a reporter.

"Jon, how do you see your role this year with the Bucks?"

Jon had come into the league a year ahead of me and was very much a role player. He was also a smart and funny guy who liked to have a good time. I considered him a friend, as well as an integral part of our posse when we went out to clubs at night. But Jon could also be a wiseass, and he had a bit of a chip on his shoulder. I suppose that comes with the territory when your dad is Rick Barry, a Hall of Famer and one of the greatest scorers in the history of the game. Anyway, Jon smiled at the question and offered this response:

"Well, my role will probably be like an old chore that my mother gave me that I really didn't like all the time, but I accepted it, and that's to feed the dog."

The comment naturally was met with laughter; Jon knew

how to tell a joke and to work a crowd. He didn't mean anything by it, and in fact there was truth in his statement. That
is precisely the role Jon would have with the Bucks: to support Glenn Robinson. For some reason, though, it bothered
me to hear him say it.

What about me, Jon? What about feeding your bro?

I was a little icy toward Jon for a while after that, and he
responded in kind. Tension mounted over the course of several weeks, and finally spilled over one day in practice when
Jon grabbed a rebound near me and swung his elbows wildly
after corralling the ball. Now, flying elbows are a part of
the game in basketball, but there is an unspoken rule among
players about when and how flagrantly they can be utilized
(there are some very clear and concise rules set down by the
NBA as well, but that is a different matter entirely). Clear-
ing space and sending a message is one thing, especially in a
game, but deliberately swinging your elbows in the vicinity
of a teammate's face in practice? That's a problem.

As we ran down the court together, I let Jon know exactly how I felt.

"Yo, JB . . . watch your 'bows, man."

Jon did not even make eye contact. Instead, as he backped-
aled, he said, "Fuck you, Vinnie. I'll do what I want to do."

From there things escalated quickly. We had passed the
point of settling our differences like adults. Now we were
like a couple of kids on the playground, where you never call
fouls and basketball games frequently devolve into fistfights.

Another missed shot, another aggressive rebound by
Jon, with me right next to him, and another flying elbow.
This one nearly clipped me in the face. Rather than passing
the ball ahead, Jon began dribbling. He raced up the court
as quickly as he could, obviously intent on trying to score

and make me look bad. So I went after him. As he crossed midcourt I caught up to him and cracked him in the back of the head with my forearm. The ball went one way, Jon and I went another. We both spilled to the floor and commenced wrestling like fools. I had seven inches and nearly fifty pounds on Jon—although I wasn't ordinarily as feisty as he was—and quickly gained the upper hand by putting him in a choke hold. Never before had I felt that much rage, and I don't even know where it came from. It was similar to the sort of thing I used to feel in college, when I would get chewed out in practice, except now I wasn't responding with tears of frustration. Now I lashed out.

"Jesus, Vinnie, get off me!" Jon screamed. "You're breaking my neck!"

I did not get off him. I did not loosen my grip until one of our assistants, Butch Carter, leaped onto my back and physically pried my fingers from Jon's throat. I rolled over, scrambled to my feet, and ran straight to the locker room, where I punched a wall and broke down in tears. I felt such a complicated swirl of emotions: anger at Jon's provocation, disappointment in myself over having nearly hurt my friend, and surprise that I had so quickly lost all composure. In general, I just felt . . . bad. I was embarrassed. But not everyone thought it was such a terrible thing. The guys on the team mostly responded with amusement. And the coaches? While they did not condone fighting among teammates, they certainly did not object to seeing laid-back Vin Baker express a more violent and aggressive side.

"Man, I'm sorry," I said through glassy eyes when Butch tracked me down. "There's no excuse for that."

Butch patted me on the back. "It's okay, Vin. Don't worry about it. Shit happens." Then he laughed, and moved in closer, so that he could almost whisper in my ear. "I'll tell you something else—you'd better not change."

I got the message, loud and clear. While no one on the coaching staff was going to advocate wrestling matches among teammates, they were not unhappy to see a little fire out of a guy who had often been branded too nice for his own good. I just had to be more consistent in channeling my anger in productive ways.

There was no lingering bad blood between JB and me. He was my boy and there was no way I was going to let a fight ruin our friendship, although I'll admit to feeling uncomfortable when we got on the team bus the next day. I thought he might be mad at me. Given the circumstances, I wouldn't have blamed him. I could have seriously hurt Jon, and if that had happened, I don't know if I could have forgiven myself. But Jon took the high road. He was one of the last players to board the bus, and I was already seated near the back. I could see him scanning the rows looking for something as he slowly made his way down the aisle. When our eyes met, he nodded and smiled, quickened his pace, and made his way to my seat. He sat down next to me. For a moment we sat in silence. Then Jon broke the ice.

"Here, bro. I got something for you." He reached into his bag and pulled out a portable DVD player. In 1994, before the advent of streaming video and iPhones and iPads, portable DVD players, with flip tops and tiny screens, were a miracle, coveted by anyone who spent long hours on the road with no easy way to fill the travel time. "I know you don't have one," Jon added. "Hope you like it."

It's not like I couldn't afford my own portable DVD player, but that wasn't the point. I didn't have one, and I had spoken admiringly of the devices owned by some of the guys on the team. I just hadn't gotten around to buying one. Jon remembered this, and took care of it for me.

"Thanks, JB," I said, before adding, "My bad about yesterday."

Jon waved a hand dismissively. "Come on, man. Whatever. Forget about it."

When Todd Day got on the bus a few minutes later and saw me playing with my new toy, he was instantly intrigued. It had been kind of a running joke on the team that I had this big contract but wouldn't spend any money. No fancy cars, no mansion, nothing. And everyone knew that I didn't do electronics. I could barely figure out the remote on the modest little TV in my apartment. So Todd was naturally surprised.

"What the hell is that?" he said.

"Oh, it's just one of those little portable DVD players."

Todd smirked. "I know what the fuck it is, man. I mean, where did you get it? You don't buy shit like that."

"Yeah, JB got it for me."

Todd did a double take, looking toward the front of the bus, then at me, then toward the front again. On his face was an expression of utter exasperation.

"What the fuck?! Who? I mean . . . you guys were trying to kill each other yesterday in practice."

I nodded. "Uh-huh."

"Damn," Todd said, shaking his head in disbelief. "I might have to beat JB, too."

"Come on, TD. Knock it off. That's not funny."

"Nah, man. I'm serious. I'm gonna kick his ass tomorrow. I need a new cell phone."

I BECAME ONE OF GLENN ROBINSON'S closest friends on the Bucks, although I can't honestly say that I got to know him all that well.
Dog was a little weird, kind of an introvert, so you couldn't
really sit around with him and have deep conversations about
stuff. We bonded first on the court; whatever jealousy I may
have harbored toward Dog because of his status as a number
one pick and franchise savior, there was no questioning the
guy's ability as a basketball player. We both viewed ourselves
as alpha males within the context of the team, and ordinarily that can present problems. But for some reason we got
along great and figured out our respective roles. I was kind
of like Scottie Pippen to Glenn's Michael Jordan. I was a star
on the Bucks; Dog was *the* star. And that was fine with me.
Dog could score like few players I had ever seen, and I felt
privileged to play alongside him. The guy was ridiculously
gifted from an offensive standpoint. I made peace very early
in Dog's tenure that he'd be our leading scorer and offensive
threat.

I could score, too, but not like Glenn. I did other things.
I could block shots and rebound. I played defense and passed
the ball. So we became boys because our stats began lining
up in a complementary fashion. We played well together
and we understood each other. It was a comfortable relationship, and it led to our hanging out a bit off the court as
well. Now, I knew that Dog liked his weed—a lot. And as
we began spending some time together I came to see that
smoking was his primary recreational activity. He didn't
drink much, didn't like to go out to clubs. He just liked to
chill at home with some friends and get high. That was his
thing, and it was one of the reasons he was considered such
an enigma.

I joined Dog on occasion, maybe once a week early in

the season. Pretty soon, once a week became twice a week. Then three times a week—in addition to going out with the guys and hitting strip clubs when we were on the road. I was drinking and smoking weed, although I wouldn't call my use of either excessive. And I was playing very good basketball, so there were no indications that I was out of control or otherwise compromising my basketball career. Just the opposite, in fact. Even as I dabbled a little more extensively with drugs and alcohol, my performance improved. I averaged 17.7 points and 10.3 rebounds per game in my second season, and was named to the NBA All-Star team for the first time. Go figure.

IT'S TEMPTING TO CONNECT DOTS that should not be connected, to look for a causal relationship where one does not exist—or where the relationship is tenuous at best—and I certainly did that where marijuana was concerned. Initially there were a few simple things I liked about smoking weed: the gentle euphoria and the slipping away of anxiety; the quiet camaraderie of hanging out with a small group of buddies, watching TV, and getting high; and the inevitable food binge that came afterward. I love eating—always have—and smoking turned me into an eating machine. And in the beginning, at least, I picked my spots carefully, smoking only on off days or after practice, and only lightly, just enough to get a little buzz. The great thing about weed is that not much is required to reach a state of mild inebriation. And hangovers are practically nonexistent. In that sense, it's a far better match for the athlete's lifestyle than alcohol is. On the downside, alcohol is predictable: you know how much you can drink, and what the effects are likely to be. Back in those days, when weed was illegal nationwide, it was a mystery: you never knew exactly what was in it, or the level of THC, or the kind of trip you might experience. You could smoke an entire joint and be only slightly buzzed, or you could take a single hit and be incapacitated. Every high was an adventure.

Knowing the risks, I abstained from marijuana for roughly twenty-four hours before a game or practice. And usually more like forty-eight hours. That was my routine, and I thought it was one embraced by just about all the guys in the league who liked to smoke. I mean, who would be crazy enough to play while high?

The answer came one day at Glenn Robinson's place, during my third season with the Bucks. I still remember the date: January 5, 1996. We had a home game scheduled that evening against the Portland Trail Blazers, so as always there was a morning shootaround. Afterward I went back to Dog's house to hang out and get a haircut (this was not uncommon—we'd hire someone to come to the house rather than going out and dealing with fans). It was just me and him and a few of his boys from back home—sometimes it seemed like Dog had half of Gary, Indiana, living with him. I don't even remember who broke out the weed. I just remember smelling it while I was getting my haircut. Out of the corner of my eye I could see the joint being passed around, and I remember feeling very curious about what would happen when it got to Glenn. By this point I knew that Dog was a heavy smoker, but I figured smoking on game day was a line you simply did not cross, no matter how much you liked weed. I tried to turn my head enough to see what was happening and got scolded by the girl cutting my hair, but I caught a glimpse of Dog taking the joint in hand, pressing it to his lips, and inhaling deeply.

What the . . . ?!

Glenn was such a good basketball player, and such a phenomenal athlete, that I couldn't imagine him taking a chance like this. But the truth is, his demeanor was so nonchalant that there was no mistaking this as anything but part of his normal game-day routine.

"Dog," I said, trying not to sound judgmental. "You smoke before games?"

He shrugged. A thin, tight-lipped smile crossed his face. I checked the clock. It was around 11:30 a.m. Game time was 7:00 p.m.; we weren't due at the arena until five o'clock. That left more than five hours for Dog to get sober. I figured it wouldn't be a problem, especially since he obviously knew what he was doing. I had no intention of taking a similar risk, but when the joint came to me, instead of waving it off and saying thanks, but no thanks . . . I hit it.

Instantly I was overcome with regret. Marijuana is like a scratch-off lottery ticket, and this time I'd hit the jackpot.

Oh, no . . . what did I just do?

The high was instantaneous and potent. I felt a surge of anxiety about getting caught when I showed up that night, so I did the logical stoner thing: I tried to squelch the anxiety by smoking even more! The joint came around and I hit it again. And again . . . and again. At least five times. I don't remember the exact number, but I do know that by the time we were through, I was wasted.

Gone, however, was the anxiety and the sense of dread about getting caught; I was too messed up to care. *Plenty of time*, Dog said. *You'll be fine.* We went out, got something to eat, and then I went back to my apartment to take a nap. I figured I'd wake up sober and rested and ready to play.

Instead, when the alarm went off at four, my head was

full and foggy. I wouldn't say I was completely inebriated, but I definitely still felt the effects. I knew the feeling intimately, and it was still lingering. I drove to the arena (that's right—one of hundreds of episodes of my driving under the influence, any one of which could have gone horribly wrong) and prepared to play. I went through my usual pregame routine: stretching, relaxing in the Jacuzzi, shooting, low-post moves—and still I was high. But you know what else? I felt comfortable. I mean, I was . . . *relaxed*. I didn't feel paranoid or anxious. I just went out and played. Oh, man, did I play! That night I had 41 points and eight rebounds, and we beat the Blazers by 17—the most lopsided victory of the season (we didn't have a lot of victories that year, let alone blowouts). It was the best game of my entire career.

Talk about validation.

The truth, of course, is that there was no correlation at all. I had the talent to put up those kinds of numbers; it just hadn't happened yet. Now it had, and in that superstitious way of all athletes, I tried to link cause with effect. It became a self-fulfilling prophecy: *I'm going to smoke weed every day . . . make it part of my pregame regimen!* I remember thinking in the middle of the game, *I've got to do this. This is what it is. This is what I've been missing!*

After that, Glenn and I became even tighter. I sought him out every day, whether we had a game or not. Seemingly overnight, I went from a casual smoker of weed to a habitual smoker. It was that fast. Maybe marijuana is not physically addictive the way opioids and alcohol are addictive—you don't experience the agony of withdrawal when you stop, but when you're used to smoking every day, and you suddenly stop, you do crave the effects; you miss the high. Whether that is a psychological or physiological addiction, I don't know, but it's real, and it can wreak havoc on your life.

Dog and I became virtually inseparable, especially on game days. After that night against Portland, I got high before every game for the remainder of the season, with one notable exception: the NBA All-Star Game, which was played in Phoenix that year. I was selected to play for the second straight year. For some reason I worried about playing high that night. It was a big game with a national television audience, and I fretted about the possibility of making an error in calibration or getting weed laced with some sort of foreign substance. Better to just play sober, I thought. I played twenty-four minutes in the All-Star Game and did not distinguish myself in any way. I had six points and two rebounds—hardly memorable numbers. I came away more convinced than ever that I was a better basketball player when I was high.

I also knew that I had crossed a barrier, and that most of the guys on the team would neither understand nor approve of my behavior. Todd Day loved weed, but I never saw him, or anyone else, get high before a game. This was just between Dog and me, and we did our best to keep it that way. I'd go to his house on game days when we were in Milwaukee; on the road I'd go to his hotel room. It was a quiet and secretive ritual. If someone knocked on the door while we were smoking—which happened quite a few times—we'd look at each other and hold our breath, as if to say, *Can't let him in. Can't let anyone else in the room.*

I think a lot of guys on the team, and probably some of the coaches, suspected that Dog was lighting up before games; it was a major component of his lifestyle, and everyone knew it. But when you're playing well—and Dog was playing very well—people tend to overlook things. That I was his partner in game-day smoking was less well known, if it was known at all. I did not share this news with anyone, out of fear that I would be exposed and branded as unprofessional. I was extremely cautious. Even when I was out drinking with the boys after a game I would not let it slip.

Nope . . . couldn't take that chance.

This was my dirty little secret. And I owned it.

6

★ ★ ★

SCARED STRAIGHT (ALMOST)

By the end of my third year, I was one of the most productive frontcourt players in the league, an acknowledged all-star who could give his team 20 points and 10 rebounds just about any night of the week. Those are the kinds of numbers that people notice and that invariably lead to a feeding frenzy in free agency. In terms of basketball, things could not have been much better. I loved the game and I was having fun playing at a level that I wasn't even sure was attainable.

I was also a total weed-head.

I rarely drank or even went out much anymore. Alcohol is a far more social drug than marijuana, in part because of its legality, but also because it works as a social lubricant. When

I would drink, I wanted to hit the clubs and be the life of the party. When I'd smoke, I just wanted to chill and hang with a couple of my boys. It didn't take long to reach the point where the sober hours were outnumbered by the inebriated hours. I hardly ever went out during this period, and when I did, I'd nurse a drink for a couple of hours, just to have it in my hand and keep people from questioning me; I didn't want to look out of place.

I'd wake and bake every single morning—literally roll over, shake the cobwebs out, and light a joint. And I'd smoke the whole thing myself. The high would carry me all the way through morning practice. After practice I'd grab something to eat, come home, smoke three or four blunts—big, fat ones—and then get something to eat. Most of this was done with Dog and some of his posse, or with a couple of my friends from home. That was the routine: just smoking and eating and playing ball. Sometimes we'd invite some girls over and have a little party at Dog's mansion. But it was all very self-contained and clandestine. I got along with all my teammates, but unlike the previous year, I rarely hung out with them on the road, and definitely not when we were home. This probably led people to think that I was more of a straight arrow than some of the other guys.

Every day began and ended with weed. I smoked to wake up, and I smoked to facilitate sleep. In the middle I smoked because . . . well . . . I liked smoking. The world was a more comfortable and manageable place when encountered through the haze of cannabis. As long as I was balling at an elite level, no one was going to ask any questions. I certainly wasn't asking any of myself. As far as I was concerned, marijuana was integral to my steadily expanding success on the court. I was calm, relaxed, confident. It was almost as if the game had slowed down, and I could see everything more clearly. Weed was the magic elixir responsible for all of this—or so I told myself. And there was no way I was going to change the routine.

There was just one little problem: I was not the savviest guy in the world when it came to procuring drugs. It's not like I had a reliable contact in Milwaukee; for the most part I counted on the largesse of friends or other guys on the team who smoked regularly. Aside from Glenn Robinson, there was no one who smoked as much weed as I did. Benoit Benjamin, a well-traveled veteran center who joined the Bucks in my third season, was also a fairly prodigious smoker, so he'd hook me up as well, but my constant nagging and pestering sometimes provoked annoyance. Just to be clear, none of us was selling weed. We all had money, and Glenn usually had plenty of weed, so he mostly didn't mind sharing. But after a while I lived in a near constant state of agitation over whether I'd have enough weed to get through the coming days. I didn't recognize this for what it was: typical drug-seeking behavior, in which the addict's life revolves around nothing so much as the restocking of his supply. To me it was no more worrisome than making sure I had the right pair of basketball shoes, or that I was properly hydrated during a workout. Weed was just another tool in the kit.

But if that tool happened to be dull, or, God forbid, missing? I would freak out. Through bad planning or other circumstances beyond my control, this happened with some regularity. We'd be on the road for a few days, my stash of weed would invariably diminish, and I'd have to run down to Glenn's room to replenish. Dog was my boy, my weed partner, but sometimes I tested his patience. Like a lot of guys who smoke copious amounts of marijuana, Glenn was fond of midday naps. More than once I interrupted him. He'd open the door, and with an annoyed expression on his face, he'd just shake his head.

"Again, Vinnie?"

"Yeah, sorry, Dog."

"All right . . . come on in."

In the same way that I would visit the team trainer for treatment of a sore ankle, I visited Dog for "medication" that would sustain my current level of play. I was an all-star getting accolades for my game, but far from thinking that weed jeopardized that status, I had become convinced that the drug facilitated and even enhanced my career.

But there was a steep price to pay, in the form of a handful of frightening episodes in which my heart began racing after I got high, and I wound up in the emergency room, on an IV drip, lying to the docs about what had happened and pretending that it was just a panic attack. I'm not talking about a minor escalation of pulse; I'm talking about something that felt like tachycardia—like I was about to have a heart attack. I started thinking about guys like Len Bias and Reggie Lewis and Hank Gathers, young men whose careers and lives were cut short by cardiac arrest. (In Bias's case, his death was a direct result of drug use.)

The first episode occurred in March 1996, prior to a game in Chicago, against the Bulls. Chicago is an easy ninety-minute drive from Milwaukee, so we usually bussed for this game. I'd been up late the night before; I set my alarm for eight o'clock (the bus was scheduled to leave at 10:00 a.m.), and smoked a joint as soon as I woke. Instantly, I knew something was wrong. Instead of the usual wave of relaxation that came over me with a morning buzz, I felt a rush of anxiety. I had trouble breathing; my heart raced so quickly and loudly that I thought it might jump out of my chest. I tried to relax.

Deep breaths . . . deep breaths. Take it easy, Vinnie.

No good.

In a desperate, amateurish manner, I tried to meditate, figuring the episode would pass soon enough. But it didn't. The symptoms escalated, to the point that I thought I might pass out or even die. My college buddy Mike was living with me at the time, so I called out to him for help.

"What's wrong, Vin?"

"I don't know. I think I might be having a heart attack. You have to get me to the hospital."

Mike helped me downstairs and drove me to the emergency room, where I was attended to quickly and dramatically. Medical personnel rushed me right past the front desk and into an examining bay before even filing out the proper paperwork. I was quickly hooked up to an array of machinery, given an IV, and peppered with questions.

"Do you have a history of heart disease?"

"No."

"Have you ever had an episode like this before?"

"No."

"Are you on any type of medication?"

"No."

And then the big one . . .

"Do you use recreational drugs, and have you taken anything today?"

Long pause . . . "No . . . never."

The docs and nurses were surprisingly calm about all of this. I presume they had heard and seen it all before; whether I was telling the truth or not was almost irrelevant. They were merely checking the appropriate boxes.

"Well, clearly something unusual is happening, Mr. Baker,

so we're going to have to keep you here for a while and monitor your condition."

They recognized me, which helped ensure a degree of discretion and privacy, or at least as much as was possible within the crowded confines of the emergency room. I appreciated the attention and sensitivity and professionalism, but I also knew that I couldn't afford to miss the bus to Chicago, as then there would be myriad questions to answer— from the coaching staff and management, from fans, and from the media. While this episode was nothing more than a panic attack, it was bound to raise eyebrows. When a team's star player winds up in the ER—for any reason—it's big news. Even as the medication coursed through my veins and slowed my heartbeat, as my mood stabilized and the anxiety faded away, and with it the fear of death by cardiac arrest, I squirmed at the prospect of public scrutiny. I felt relatively normal and wanted to get out of the hospital as quickly as possible, before anyone on the Bucks got word of the episode.

After an hour or so, I told the attending physician that I wanted to leave. The doctor strongly discouraged me, suggested a full battery of tests, and perhaps an overnight stay in the hospital.

"This is not something to take lightly, Mr. Baker," he said. "We want to be sure you're all right."

"I'm fine, believe me." Then I proceeded to spin a convincing yarn about previous anxiety attacks and similar episodes with benign outcomes. The doc was sympathetic, but ultimately unconvinced. I kept looking at my watch, insisting I'd be okay.

"I have a game to play tonight, Doc. I really have to go."

In the end, the hospital declined discharge. If I were to have had a heart attack two hours after being released from the ER with a clean bill of health, the hospital would have been liable. Prudence on their part demanded further testing. Prudence on my part was something else: I had to leave. So I signed something known as a Discharge Against Medical Advice (DAMA) form, which provided legal absolution to the hospital. I thanked everyone for their kindness and professionalism, and walked out. Mike drove me to the arena, where I caught the bus to Chicago without anyone's being the wiser. I went through shootaround without incident, got something to eat, and took a nap.

And then I got high in my hotel room before the game.

That night I had 21 points and eight rebounds in a nine-point loss to the Bulls. Three nights later, in Atlanta, I had 34 points and 10 rebounds against the Hawks, and two nights after that I had 25 and 12 against the Celtics. It was one of the most productive three-game stretches of my career, and it came on the heels of what felt like a near-death experience. And I was stoned for every minute of each game.

I'm sure some of my teammates in Milwaukee suspected there was an issue. Terry Cummings, for example, would occasionally give me a sideways glance during practice . . . a look that seemed to say, *Son, there's something going on here.* But he wouldn't put his thoughts into words; it was just something I felt, probably because Terry was such a clean-cut, thoughtful guy.

Armen Gilliam, another of my teammates on the Bucks, would also toss subtle hints my way: a look of concern, for example, or an inquiry, out of the blue, about how I was feeling. Armen never confronted me personally, but he did talk to my father once. I resented it at the time, of course—that's what addicts do; they get pissed off when people try to help.

My output continued to improve, despite my best efforts

at sabotage. I averaged 21.1 points and 9.9 rebounds that season, played in the All-Star Game again, and generally continued to perform like one of the league's top centers. In the summer, though, came another frightening episode related to smoking weed. Much like the previous time, the effects were instantaneous. I took a hit, and my heart started racing. But this one was even worse. My chest felt constricted; I was light-headed.

Oh, man . . . this time it really is a heart attack.

I was alone and had to drive myself to the hospital. I raced through the streets of Milwaukee—flying through red lights and stop signs at fifty, sixty miles an hour. Other drivers leaned on their horns as cars jumped out of the way. I felt like I was going to black out behind the wheel. I gripped even tighter as I tried to take slow, shallow breaths.

Hang on . . . hang on . . .

At the hospital—the same hospital, incidentally—there was much commotion, just as there had been a few months earlier. Same set of questions, same denials on my part, and the same nonjudgmental response from the doctors. This time, however, I was in no hurry to leave. I stayed for several hours, went through a battery of tests, and ultimately was determined to have suffered nothing more serious than a panic attack. They released me with what amounted to the following recommendation:

Try to relax.

I couldn't relax. Whether for physiological or psychological reasons, my response to smoking had become dangerous and unpredictable. Could I play without weed? Could I even get through the day without it?

I had no idea.

I spent a lot of time that summer training with Glenn

Robinson. Two or three times a week we'd get together at the Cousins Center, where the Bucks practiced, and work out. The sessions were intense and productive, except on those occasions when I felt dazed and confused. This happened with greater frequency as the summer stretched on; instead of getting in better shape, I was regressing. I had trouble breathing. My legs were heavy and sore. Sometimes I'd get light-headed after just a few minutes of warming up. On the worst days, my heart would begin racing. Then it would slow down. Then it would race again. I could feel my pulse in my throat, as if my heart were trying to climb out of my body.

It was at once disgusting and terrifying. At the end of one of those sessions I decided that I had to stop smoking weed.

"I'm done," I said to Glenn.

He smiled, laughed a little.

"Sure you are, bro."

I was 100 percent serious. I quit—not quite cold turkey, but pretty close. By the time the season started I had cut way back on weed, and by the middle of the season I had stopped completely. But I didn't get sober. I just traded one drug for another.

7

★ ★ ★

A NEW HOME IN SEATTLE

I was young and strong and improving with each passing season. I made the All-Star team three consecutive times in Milwaukee, from 1995 through 1997, but the Bucks remained a mediocre (or just plain bad), small-market franchise, and in that scenario everyone is trade bait. In the summer of 1997, after months of trying to renegotiate my contract, I was sent to the Seattle SuperSonics in a complicated three-team deal. Tyrone Hill and Terrell Brandon went to the Bucks, and Shawn Kemp and Sherman Douglas went from Seattle to the Cleveland Cavaliers.

The night that trade was announced, I drank to oblivion. And then I continued to drink the next day . . . and the day after that. A three-day binge of epic drinking. I remember

going back to my condo on the last night and watching
SportsCenter on ESPN, and thinking, *Whoa, I'm taking Shawn
Kemp's place in Seattle?* Shawn was a superstar—talented but
troubled. I found it hard to think of myself as being on the
same level as a player like that. I knew there would be expectations in Seattle that I hadn't experienced in Milwaukee.

A couple of days later I met with the Sonics' coach,
George Karl. Man, I love that guy. He is a players' coach, and
he had all the faith in the world in me. The truth was, even
though I was a three-time all-star, I was not a winner—not
in college, and not in the pros. Being an all-star was cool. It
got me a sneaker deal and it was great for the résumé. But
when you win, there is another level of fame and, especially,
respect. Guys like Michael Jordan, Larry Bird, Kobe Bryant, and Scottie Pippen—they're admired not just for their
individual accomplishments, but also for the number of rings
they've acquired. You score a bunch of points, play in the
All-Star Game, but fail to win a title? Then you're Allen
Iverson.

I knew there was a chance I'd be traded, but Seattle was
the last place I expected to land. I was a big fan of Shawn
Kemp, and now here I was, trying to take his place.

"You're my guy," Coach Karl told me. "You're the player
we want."

Everything about Seattle was different. There were big
personalities and big expectations. At the very first team
meeting, George said we should win thirty-five games at
home (and sixty games overall). Considering we played only
forty-one home games, this was one hell of a prognostica-
tion. In Milwaukee the previous year, we hadn't even won
thirty-five games *total*.

Interestingly, Shawn Kemp and I actually had a few

things in common. In addition to playing the same position, we both had issues with substance abuse (mine were less well known than Shawn's at the time.) Moreover, each of us had been traded, following protracted and unsuccessful contract negotiations. Like me, Shawn had basically been shipped off because he was unhappy with his deal. Wally Walker, the general manager of the Sonics, thought that it was probably best to move on from Shawn given some of his off-court issues, combined with financial considerations. And I kind of fit neatly with the new plan. I was a slightly younger, less experienced version of Shawn; the front office personnel and coaches love the word "potential," and on paper, at least, I seemed to be a player loaded with that particular commodity. My numbers were improving every season. I had come from a mid-major college program, so it was understood that my development would be a bit slower. No longer a detriment, this was now seen as an attribute. After seven years in the league, with some documented trouble off the court, Shawn was viewed as a player whose best years might be in the rearview mirror. Me? You could argue that I had barely scratched the surface.

Trepidation turned to excitement almost as soon as I arrived. There is a honeymoon period following these types of transactions. Fans and management are excited about the new player, and the player is excited about getting a fresh start. I quickly fell in love with the Sonics, and the feeling seemed to be mutual. During my first month or so in town I kept a low profile, worked hard, and generally just tried to fit in. I continued to abstain from marijuana, and hardly drank at all. I was fit and healthy and eager to prove that the Sonics had made the right decision (equally motivating was the prospect of proving to the Bucks that they had made a bad decision). Part of that process was earning the respect of my new teammates. For all I knew, the Sonics may have loved Shawn Kemp and resented my taking his place. Professional basketball is a business, first and foremost, and winning will solve a lot of problems. But every locker room is a fragile little ecosystem, and the sudden addition or subtraction of a key element can have serious consequences.

MOST OF MY CONCERNS WERE allayed one day before practice during the preseason. In walked the Sonics point guard Gary Payton, a big smile on his face. I didn't know a lot about GP at the time, except that he was a bona fide superstar and one of the most respected players in the game. Born and raised in Oakland (which is worth about a million points on the "tough guy" scale), Gary had been an all-American at Oregon State and was the number two overall pick in the 1990 NBA draft. By the time I got to Seattle, Gary was already a four-time NBA all-star (on his way to nine), and a member of the 1996 US Olympic team. A ferocious competitor, Gary was one of the league's all-time great defenders, as well as one of the all-time great trash-talkers. At six foot four and 185 pounds, he was long and rangy, with quick hands and an even quicker first step to the basket. Physically, Gary did not appear to be intimidating, except from the neck up. With a shaved head and a perpetual scowl, Gary was the epitome of nastiness on the court. He backed down from absolutely no one. And now that Shawn Kemp was gone, this team was his. If you wanted to fit in with the Sonics, you needed Gary's approval.

So there I was, watching him walk toward me, smiling and shaking his head theatrically.

Oh, man . . . GP's got me in his sights. What's he gonna do?

"Yo, Vinnie!" he shouted. "You missed it, man. Steve shouted you out last night."

"Steve who?"

Gary rolled his eyes, like I'd asked the stupidest question.

"Steve, man. Steve Harvey."

Back in those days Steve Harvey was less a talk show personality or game show host than a stand-up comic. GP was a big fan of Steve's, so naturally when his tour passed through Seattle, Gary was in attendance.

"What do you mean he shouted me out?" I asked.

"He said, 'Hey, it's crazy what the Sonics just did, huh? You guys got rid of the devil and brought in a preacher!'"

Gary laughed, long and hard; so did everyone else within earshot. I just sort of stood there, the discomfort coursing through my body. On one hand, I was relieved to know that my new teammates found this funny—maybe they really were happy to see Shawn go. On the other hand, I didn't really like being contrasted to Shawn in this way. I had admired Shawn as a player and sympathized with his off-court struggles. There were issues with drugs and alcohol, there were multiple paternity suits (during my first year in Seattle, it would be revealed that Shawn had fathered at least fourteen children with thirteen different women). By comparison, at the time, I was a choirboy, if not exactly a preacher, but I knew that I had flirted with disaster. I'd played more than a hundred games while high, so I certainly wasn't going to throw any stones. I had a chance to start over in Seattle, with one of the league's most esteemed franchises, and a smart coach who was happy to have me on his team.

I nodded at Gary. "Funny guy."

Life with the Sonics differed in ways that extended beyond the court. For one thing, I discovered right away that there was a lot of heavy drinking among players. Some guys smoked weed, too, but there was a small and dedicated group of partiers—guys who liked to go out after games, at home and on the road, and really cut loose, even more so than we had in Milwaukee. I was a casual drinker when I first got to Seattle, semi-intent on cleaning up my act, but quickly became one of the boys. And the leader of the boys was Gary Payton. On the basketball court he was relentlessly antagonistic and ornery, but off the floor I discovered that Gary was a lot of fun to be around, and we quickly became good friends.

He also was a prodigious drinker. I've never seen anyone who could drink like Gary and seem to be unaffected. It was otherworldly. When I got to Seattle, I was almost in awe of Gary (despite the fact that he was only a couple of years older than me), but once we started drinking together, it kind of put us on the same level. For all the reasons that I had started drinking in Milwaukee, I resumed heavy drinking in Seattle. My energy was different. I was comfortable, less anxious.

And Gary noticed.

"Man, you ain't Old Saybrook," he'd say. "You kinda Oakland."

This was exactly what Coach Karl and the Sonics had wanted when they traded for me—not the drinking, but a young player (younger than Kemp) who would not only perform on the court, but would also be likable and would bond with his teammates; a positive addition to the locker room environment. And GP ran that locker room. What Gary discovered was that Shawn and I were on basically the same level as players, but that I could hang with him, too.

In Seattle it was just fun, both on and off the court. Coach Karl is an interesting guy. He knows how to motivate and he really knows the game from a technical standpoint. He's had issues with some players over the years, and with some front office people, which doesn't really surprise me. Back then, at least, George was an extremely confident guy; his confidence bordered on cockiness or even arrogance, although in a good sort of way. George had been knocked around a bit in his career, but the experience only seemed to make him stronger. He was a Dean Smith disciple, having played at North Carolina before spending five years with the San Antonio Spurs. When his playing days were over, George slid right into coaching, first as an assistant with the Spurs, and then as head coach of the Montana Golden Nuggets of the Continental Basketball Association. The CBA was minor-league ball, but George proved he could coach there by twice reaching the finals and twice being named CBA coach of the year.

For this he was rewarded with a promotion to the NBA. He spent a couple of tumultuous years with the Cleveland Cavaliers, and then two more with the Golden State Warriors before resigning near the end of the 1988–89 season. Then he bounced between the CBA and the European professional leagues for four years, always winning far more games than he lost, before finally making it back to the NBA in 1992, as head coach of the Sonics. I think George gained a lot of perspective about dealing with both coaches and front office personnel during his travels, and he remained one of the most competitive guys I have ever known.

I was excited to play for George. I thought he would make me better, and I felt like we had a good chance to win a title. I came away from those early meetings and practices with the unmistakable impression that the Sonics felt they had gotten the better part of the deal, and I wanted to prove them right.

Gary Payton had something to prove as well: that he could

be the leader on one of the NBA's best teams, and could carry that team to a championship despite the departure of an acknowledged superstar. So, we had that in common. Each of us was playing with a chip on his shoulder. Coach Karl had said something to me about how Gary and Shawn never really had the type of relationship that he, as a coach, wanted them to have. Their personalities simply didn't mesh well.

"Same as you and Glenn Robinson in Milwaukee," George opined. "But you and Gary? This could be great."

Dog and I worked well together in Milwaukee—we just didn't have enough supporting players to be a strong team. You need talent as well as chemistry to win in the NBA, and the Bucks had too little of both. Although Glenn appeared laconic and isolated to outsiders, and I was perceived as social but relatively straight, we were practically attached at the hip. There was also the perception that both Gary and I (me more than Gary) had not fully blossomed because of the long shadows cast by our more famous teammates. And so we met at a time when we were both trying to establish our identities. Milwaukee had basically said to me, *You're not a winner and we're tired of losing with you.* Meanwhile, Seattle was saying to Gary, *Let's see you win without Shawn.*

Each of us knew that the other felt pressure. It could have been a disastrous pairing, but it worked for reasons I had not anticipated, and that the Sonics probably did not expect. We didn't have to discuss it. We just knew that the eyes of basketball fans in Seattle, and throughout the league, were going to be on us. Could Gary Payton lead this team to sixty wins? And could Vin Baker be part of a winning team? We were considered complementary players (point guard and center/power forward), as well as complementary personalities: Gary's dad was Al Payton, a legend in Oakland basketball circles who went by the nickname "Mr. Mean." Gary picked up his own nickname—"the Glove," because of his tenacity on the defensive end of the floor—but he may just as well have been "Mr. Mean Jr." Sometimes his desire to win would collide with his generally temperamental nature, resulting in dustups not merely with opposing players, but also with his own teammates and coaches. All of this was overstated, in my opinion—just as it was understated about me. ESPN did a feature on the two of us that first season, focusing not only on the way we meshed on the court, but also on what was perceived to be an unlikely friendship. I can still see one of our teammates, Hersey Hawkins, looking into the camera and smiling, and describing our partnership this way: "I guess opposites attract."

That was the popular notion in those days, and while there may have been a kernel of truth to it, the reality was this: Gary and I had more in common than anyone realized. I may have been the son of a preacher, but, like Gary, I could also be a son of a bitch. The transformation did not come as easily to me as it did to Gary, but it was real, and it was lurking just beneath the surface. The ability to summon that persona on demand, rather than melt into a puddle of tears when provoked, as I had when I was younger, was critical to my development as an athlete. Like Gary, I had been raised by tough, demanding parents; my dad may not have been called Mr. Mean, but there was certainly a time when that nickname would not have been inappropriate.

As for our respective reputations off the court? Gary was known to be a guy who liked going out after games and hitting the clubs, but it never seemed to affect his ability to play, so not much was made of it. Even a daily weed smoker wouldn't draw much attention so long as he continued to perform well on game days.

I had no long-term plans when I got to Seattle. I figured I would play out the remainder of my contract and then test the waters of free agency. If everything went well with the Sonics, maybe they'd be willing to dig deep into their pockets to keep me there. But there were no guarantees. I spent the first month in a hotel, then rented a house in a nice suburban area near Cougar Mountain. (True story—I was told that the Seattle Mariners pitcher Randy Johnson lived down the street, which for some reason was a huge selling point to me. In all the time I lived there, I never saw Randy. But it was a nice neighborhood.) My college buddy Mike, who had spent a lot of time with me in Milwaukee as well, moved in with me. He was pretty happy with this turn of events, since his girlfriend, a former soccer player at the University of Hartford, was already living in Seattle. And, obviously, Seattle is just a beautiful place, truly one of the most livable cities in the United States.

The first couple of months in Seattle were all business. I worked my butt off to fit in and present a serious, professional image. I could tell right away from our pickup games that I was going to enjoy playing for the Sonics. I'd heard a lot about how Western Conference basketball was different from Eastern Conference ball, but until I got to Seattle I thought it was mostly just a matter of perspective and reputation. There really were fundamental differences, though, in philosophy and style of play. East Coast teams played a more deliberate style of game: walk the ball up the floor, run the half-court offense to death, pound the boards, use your fists and elbows when necessary, lots of dirty work on defense. The East was the home of the Celtics, Bulls, and, especially, the Detroit Pistons—whose "Bad Boys" teams of the nineties featured such noted tough guys as Bill Laimbeer, Dennis Rodman, and Isaiah Thomas. I'd played in the East, so I knew what it was like: low and slow. I didn't mind, because I was a low-post ballplayer and much of what we ran in Milwaukee went through me. Lots of touches, plenty of chances to score.

In Seattle I discovered there was another way to play basketball, one that did not necessarily revolve around the half-court offense, and therefore might not mean as many opportunities for me, but which was a whole lot more fun to execute. The West, after all, was the home of the LA Lakers, the "Showtime" Lakers of Magic Johnson and James Worthy, of Kareem and Kobe and Shaq. It was all about running and pushing the pace of the game: get the rebound, make the outlet pass, fill the lanes, spread the floor. Everyone was expected to run and to score; there was less emphasis on specific positions, and more focus on simply playing basketball. Forget about backing the ball down, forget about double-teams in the post and kicking the ball out. This was like a controlled version of pickup ball, like being a kid back on the playground, where you played for the sheer joy of the game. In Milwaukee I had begun the process of adapting to an old man's game. Centers and power forwards can play a long time in the NBA because they do not run as much. They get beat up inside, in the paint, but their legs take less pounding than the legs of a smaller man. Fewer miles on the engine result in a longer professional life. But I wasn't worried about that. I was still young (just twenty-six when I arrived in Seattle), and I quickly discovered that I could get up and down the floor with the best of them.

"Coach, I am made for this," I said one day to George Karl, a trace of incredulity in my voice.

George smiled. "Yes, you are."

There were other differences as well. Coach Karl was

calm and confident. George was in charge and we all knew it. There was no need for him to beat his chest or impose silly rules as a way to demonstrate authority. George would even sometimes open practices to the friends and family of his players, which was unheard of with the Bucks (and with many teams, I would imagine). I can remember looking over at my buddy Mike during an early practice and smiling in disbelief as he sat courtside, quietly watching us run through drills.

"Can you believe this?" I said as I ran past him. Mike just shrugged.

It goes without saying that even up-tempo ball isn't a lot of fun if you're not winning games, and in order to win games, you need talent. While I was considered a significant acquisition for the Sonics, I did not have to shoulder the burden of being a franchise player, or at least not the only franchise player. In addition to GP and Hersey Hawkins, a high-scoring shooting guard, the Sonics returned the veteran forwards Sam Perkins and Detlef Schrempf and shooting guard Dale Ellis. Gone were Shawn Kemp's 19 points and 10 rebounds per game, but my numbers were nearly identical (a little higher, actually), so we were okay in that regard. It was a strong team with an interesting and eclectic mix of players, with a very good coach on the bench. Although George's prediction of winning sixty games spooked me a bit at first, I came to accept it as an ambitious but attainable goal. And when we added two solid players in point guard Greg Anthony and the small forward Jerome Kersey fairly early in the season, we got even stronger. A championship run seemed possible.

Chemistry is so important to a team, and we had it in abundance. By "chemistry," I don't necessarily mean that everyone hung out together all the time. I'm talking about assembling a group of professionals who like and respect each other, and who are able to work toward a common goal, regardless of their similarities and differences. Gary was a big personality, and very intense. You want a guy like that on your team, but you don't necessarily want six or seven guys like that, because they'll tear each other apart. Too many alpha dogs is not a good thing. Detlef was a terrific shooter and fundamentally sound, but he was a quiet man. Same with Sam Perkins. I could be quiet or gregarious, depending on the situation and the climate, so I got along with everyone. I could go out to a club with Gary or read the Bible with Hersey Hawkins, who was a devout Christian. I'd been deep in both worlds, and I was comfortable in both. After four years in Milwaukee, where losing was part of the culture, I felt blessed to be in Seattle, where winning was not a dream, but an expectation, and where everyone seemed fully committed to the greater good.

Things would end badly for me in Seattle, through no one's fault but my own, but I learned a lot while I was there about the value of teamwork, of shared responsibility and sacrifice, and of embracing diversity.

In Seattle my focus changed and I became the basketball player I had always wanted to be: a player who could not only stuff the stat sheet—I'd been doing that since high school and didn't have a single championship to show for it—but also help make his teammates better. In the process, maybe we'd achieve something close to greatness; maybe we'd compete for an NBA title. I believed that with all my heart. And from the very first practice I tried to prove it. I came through the door and kicked ass. I tried to grab every rebound, block every shot.

I was in the best shape of my life. Not since I first came into the NBA had I been so completely immersed in the game. Back then I was just happy to be a pro, and to be getting paid for playing a game I loved. After four years of losing basketball in Milwaukee, I wanted something more. I wanted to be part of something bigger. Now that was within reach.

8

★ ★ ★

EGO GETS IN THE WAY

t took only one month of the 1997–98 season for an NBA
narrative to emerge: the Seattle Sonics were the best team
in the Western Conference and perhaps the best team in
the league. We were 13–3 at the end of November, with a
signature victory over Michael Jordan and the Chicago Bulls,
who were the defending NBA champs. I had 19 points and
12 rebounds that night, hit the game-winning shot, and then
blocked a potential game winner by Toni Kukoc at the other
end as time ran out.

Looking back on it now, I can honestly say that game
was among the high points of my entire career, and it came
just as I was beginning to slip back into a pattern of heavy

drinking—not every night, mind you, but two, three, even four times a week. Still, I was so young and fit that it took a while for the effects to become noticeable. And we kept winning, which tends to deflect all manner of criticism.

In January we traveled to Cleveland for a game against the Cavaliers. Ordinarily, a nonconference game in the dead of winter would not provoke a lot of excitement, but this one created some buzz. We were on a roll at the time, leading the Western Conference with an eye-popping record of 27–6. I mean, we were just killing people. For a team that had added a lot of new pieces, we were playing with an impressive amount of chemistry. Just about every night I'd think back to what Coach Karl had said about his expectations for the season, and how initially I had wondered if the bar was set too high. Now it seemed to be positioned at precisely the appropriate level.

Cleveland, meanwhile, had improved significantly and was now one of the better teams in the East, thanks in part to the arrival of Shawn Kemp. The Cavs were 20–11, only a couple of games behind the Bulls in the Central Division, and Shawn led the team in both scoring and rebounding. The media handled the buildup to this game in predictable fashion, focusing on the fact that it would be Shawn's first opportunity to play against the team that had cut him loose, and it was my first opportunity to play against the team's former star. During shootaround that morning we walked through our offensive sets, talked about various matchups, and generally mapped out a game plan. Nothing out of the ordinary. But when we began talking about defensive assignments, Dwane Casey, one of our assistant coaches, said something that surprised me.

"Hey, V, you're over here; you'll be guarding Ilgauskas."

He was referring to Zydrunas Ilgauskas, the Cavs' seven-foot-three Lithuanian center, a mountain of a man and a handful for any defender, but let's face it—not nearly the player that Shawn Kemp was.

"Case, I'm not on Shawn?"

Dwane shook his head. "Nah, it's no big deal, Vin. We just want to make sure we've got him under control and keep you out of foul trouble."

This was not the truth. I could tell by Dwane's demeanor and body language—he seemed uncomfortable, almost nervous—that other forces were in play. Were they worried that Shawn, motivated by revenge, was going to come out and have the game of his life? Did they think I'd overcompensate in an effort to prove that the Sonics had made the right decision? Were they concerned about a possible altercation between Shawn and me? Regardless of the intent, I interpreted the message this way:

They aren't quite over this guy.

The idea that Shawn was some sort of boogeyman seemed ridiculous to me. We were the best team in the NBA at that time, and there was no reason to put so much emphasis on one player, even if he was a former teammate. The truth, however, is that teams often are careful about how they handle trades and acquisitions, and the inevitable confrontations that subsequently arise. Generally speaking, when you trade a player, especially a very good player, you prefer to deal with a team from a different conference, so that you don't have to compete against him very often. This is why I ended up in Seattle and Shawn wound up in Cleveland; I went East to West, and he went West to East. But when you do face a former player, it's not unusual for a coach to be judicious about defensive assignments. Two players who were involved in a trade sometimes get emotional and take things personally, and that can be bad for everyone involved.

There was no reason to worry. We opened up a twenty-point lead in the first quarter and rolled to our seventh straight victory. The final score was 109–84. Shawn was largely ineffective: nine points on just 2-for-11 shooting, and only six rebounds. It wasn't for lack of effort, and I honestly don't think he was spooked or nervous about playing his old team. We were just that much better than the Cavs. We doubled Shawn on nearly every possession, forced the Cavs to get output from other players, and it simply didn't happen. The game was over almost as soon as it started. I finished with 25 points and seven rebounds in just twenty-eight minutes of playing time. A very solid game, and I was happy with my performance. But it's a lot easier to play well, and to look good, when you are surrounded by guys who know how to play the game, and when you have a smart coach on the bench. We had all of this in Seattle.

By the All-Star Break we had a record of 37–10—right on pace to finish as the best team in the Western Conference and challenge for an NBA title. We won four straight games heading into the break, the last coming at home against the Indiana Pacers, who were leading the Eastern Conference with a record of 33–13. I'd already been picked to play in the All-Star Game for the fourth consecutive year, but this time felt different; this time I was part of a winning team. I was proud as hell to represent the Sonics, and I wanted to perform well on that stage. And I thought I would, especially since I played one of my very best games against the Pacers: a career-high 41 points and 11 rebounds in a 104–97 victory. One of the proudest moments of my life occurred that night, when in the postgame press conference the Pacers' coach, Larry Bird, said,

"There were times tonight when I was wishing that Shawn Kemp was back on the floor."

Larry Bird was one of the greatest players in NBA history. In the late 1970s and throughout the 1980s, fans marveled at the exploits of Bird. He was six nine but had the court vision and passing ability of a point guard; his shooting range knew no boundaries. He was routinely labeled as "unathletic," but that's just because he was white and didn't dunk very often. If you understood basketball, you knew that Larry Bird played the game in a way that it had rarely been played before. He was also a notorious trash-talker and one of the most competitive players in league history. For me, a kid growing up in New England, there was no debate. Larry was the leader of the Boston Celtics, and I was a die-hard Celtics fan. It was surreal to have praise heaped on me by my childhood hero.

Larry Legend? Talking about me? My career could have ended right there and I would have been a happy man.

THE 1998 ALL-STAR GAME SHOULD have been a terrific experience. I had been playing well, and I felt like I deserved my place on the roster. Even better, since Seattle had the best record in the Western Conference, George Karl was selected as coach. But as the All-Star weekend approached, I realized that there was something dramatically wrong with my body. It's not unusual to feel tired at the midpoint of an NBA season, especially when you're playing a lot of minutes, as I had been. But this was different. I was completely and utterly exhausted. Rather than mere soreness or fatigue, it felt like a systemic breakdown, the origins of which could easily be traced back to the way I was living my life off the court.

The All-Star Game was in New York that year, so naturally the spotlight was a bit brighter than usual. It sure felt
different to me. I remember walking into a press conference,
accompanied by a member of the NBA public relations staff
who had been assigned specifically to me (that had never
happened before), and running into Tim Hardaway of the
Miami Heat, who was not only one of the top point guards
in the league, but also one of its biggest personalities. When
it came to filling a room, Hardaway was right up there with
Jordan and GP.

"There he is, there he is," Tim shouted at me. "We saw
that forty-one the other night, bro. But we got something for
you in this game, V. We got Zo."

"Zo," of course, was Alonzo Mourning, Hardaway's Mi-
ami teammate and an all-star in his own right. And this time
I didn't mind hearing my name in the same sentence as his.
In fact, it felt pretty damn good. Four consecutive All-Star
Games, but no one had ever treated me like this before, and
it was all about the fact that I was now on a winning team.
With winning came not just acceptance, but respect. I was
part of the club now, in every way imaginable.

I realize how this makes me sound: insecure, anxious,
immature. Truth be told, all those adjectives were entirely
applicable at that point in my life, and for some time afterward. Insecurity and a lack of self esteem often fuel the engine of addiction, and certainly this was true in my case. I
liked the attention that came with being a star athlete. I also
liked the way I felt when I indulged in the fringe benefits of
that stardom.

In New York, I did not miss an opportunity to party.
The game was Sunday afternoon, and our first official practice was Saturday morning. I was out very late Friday night,

clubbing and drinking and having a good time. I wasn't alone in this behavior, but I was alone in failing to answer the bell Saturday morning.

There was a knock on my hotel room door from one of the assistant coaches. I could hear his voice outside.

"Vin, you okay?"

I sat up in bed and instantly felt the first unmistakable signs of a hangover: the headache, the nausea. Not terrible, but enough to know that it would not be a good day. Or at least not a good morning.

"Yeah, yeah, what's up?" I answered.

"You're late, man. Whole team is downstairs. Bus leaving. We're waiting on you."

I threw on my workout gear and some cologne to mask the smell, and staggered to the elevator. When I got on the bus to drive us to practice, I had to walk past a gauntlet of future Hall of Fame players: Shaquille O'Neal, Kobe Bryant, Karl Malone, just to name a few. They all knew I'd been out the night before, so they beat me up pretty good, but not in a nasty way. We were all adults, after all, and the All-Star Game was supposed to be a fun weekend. The coaches said nothing, just let me take my seat and nurse my hangover. This was not something that ever would have happened to me when I was an all-star in Milwaukee; I was always the first guy on the bus, staring wide eyed at the other stars, thinking, *Wow, I can't believe I'm even here.* Now I was taking it for granted. Now I was the guy so arrogant (or troubled) that he couldn't even remember to set the alarm? Or so drunk that he didn't hear it? It hurt to even think about it.

Sufficiently chastened, and still feeling like crap, I decided to just chill in my hotel room the night before the All-Star Game. But on game day I noticed something was wrong. I felt lethargic, almost a step slower than I had been all season. It was a significant and rather sudden change after playing the best basketball of my life for the previous three and a half months. Coach Karl did his best to get me into the flow of the game, calling plays for me, trying to get teammates to feed me the ball in the post. But I didn't have it. I made just three of twelve field goal attempts in twenty-one minutes of playing time. I finished with eight points, and although I did manage to grab a respectable eight rebounds, it was not the type of performance that was expected of me, especially coming off a 41-point effort just a few days earlier.

There was no outside criticism afterward. The All-Star Game is a funky event—different teammates, coaches, styles, playing time—and it's not unusual for even the best of players to perform below their usual standards. It's mainly about having fun and celebrating the game. It's a game for the fans. Still, I knew in my heart that something was wrong. I had never suffered through a two-day hangover before, so maybe that was the cause.

Although the statistical slip was at first barely noticeable, I struggled both mentally and physically in the second half of the season. The game did not come easily to me, the way it had prior to the All-Star Break. I was tired, less focused. The Sonics continued to win, and I finished the regular season averaging 19.2 points and eight rebounds per game. A slight dip from the previous year in Milwaukee, but still very strong, and completely acceptable given the fact that we won 61 games and were rewarded with the top seed in the Western Conference playoffs.

To the casual observer, everything seemed just fine in Seattle. But things were far from fine in my head. Throughout the stretch I partied heavily—a consistent three or four nights per week. Rarely did I string nights together, mainly because the sessions were so long and debilitating that I needed time to recover. GP was almost always my partner in crime, although between us we'd usually have a posse of eight or nine guys—Gary's friends from Oakland, and mine from Hartford. Gary used to get on the team bus, pause as he strolled past my seat, and give me a hard look. He'd wait until everyone was listening, and then make some big pronouncement about the previous evening's activities.

"Yo, this motherfucker is crazy!"

The rest of our teammates would just stare in disbelief, like it was a joke or something.

"Really? Vin?"

It was like I had two different personalities: one that I presented to the public, and one that I revealed only after I'd been drinking. Gary made a habit of reminding me that I was a hypocrite. I used to read the Bible on the team bus or plane, and I wore a rubber bracelet inscribed with the message WHAT WOULD JESUS DO? Gary would walk into the gym after one of our late-night strip club sessions, and throw an arm around my shoulder. Then he'd reach down, snap the bracelet with two fingers, and laugh sarcastically.

"G, what are you doing?" I'd say.

"What? You gonna get mad at me?" Gary would respond. Then he'd scowl. "You're not even living that life. The nerve of you to try to get pissed off about this right now. It's laughable, man."

There was no bullshitting Gary. Whatever faults he may have had, the man was totally honest and transparent. He played hard—on and off the court—and made no excuses for his behavior. He also had a unique ability to turn it on and off. Unlike me, he seemed unaffected by the partying. And if he felt a need to slow down for a while, he could just do it.

I wanted to be like GP: confident, outgoing, the life of the party. The thing is, Gary was always that way—sober or drunk. Me? I needed alcohol to become a happier person. I used to tell Gary that I thought of him as my big brother. I needed his respect, his admiration, his love. I know it sounds crazy and twisted, but when we were out getting drunk, throwing money at strippers and having sex with women we barely knew, I felt closer to Gary than to anyone else I had ever known. At the time, that relationship was the most important one in my life.

THE BEST PLAYERS HAVE AN uncanny ability to focus, and never let anything get in the way of their work. I was not at that level. That same year, I was offered my own signature shoe. I was already a Nike client, but now I was going to be part of the Jordan line, with a shoe known as . . . the Vindicator. Nike wanted me to fly to Chicago for the launch, and to film a commercial, but we were scheduled to play a game at home the next night against the Utah Jazz, with whom we were fighting at the time for supremacy in the Western Conference, while positioning for the playoffs. Wally Walker, the Sonics' general manager, was at first opposed to my leaving, which was understandable. I'd have to fly by private jet to Chicago, put in a twelve-hour day filming and meeting with Nike execs, get a few hours of sleep, and fly back the next day. And waiting for me that night would be Karl Malone, one of the greatest power forwards in the history of the game.

But I wanted the gig and the notoriety that came with it, so I urged my agent, David Falk, to throw some muscle around. Which he did. That trip was a serious boost to the ego; it was also a reality check. Let me explain. See, when I first got to Chicago and met with all the Nike bigwigs, and hung out with a bunch of other superstar athletes, I felt pretty good about myself.

I'm ballin' now!

Eventually, though, I walked onto the set to film the commercial, and in walked MJ himself: Michael Jordan. I expected a handshake or a bro hug—something warm and fuzzy and emblematic of my being part of this elite club. Instead, Michael walked right up to me, looked me dead in the eye, and solemnly said, "What the hell are you doing here?"

At first I thought it was a joke, like he was busting my balls for some reason. Uh-uh. He was dead serious.

"You got a big game tomorrow, right? Shouldn't you be at practice?"

I didn't know what to say. To me it was unfathomable, and rather embarrassing, that Michael not only seemed to know more about my schedule than I did, but that he took it more seriously. That's one of the things that separate someone like Michael from other athletes: his work ethic. Despite all the fame and adulation and wealth, he never lost sight of the fact that winning was the most important thing, and winning requires enormous sacrifice and ambition. I came to Chicago filled with excitement over being asked to join the Jordan stable. Now, here I was, face to face with the man himself, and suddenly I was ashamed. All I could think was, *I am not even close to being on your level.*

THE SONICS WERE THE TOP seed in the Western Conference, a reward for having won more than sixty games during the regular season. In reality, though, by playoff time we were not as good a team as we had been earlier in the year. Timing is everything, and in a long NBA season it's not unusual for a team that plays well in the early going to struggle in the play-offs. That's what happened to us, and I will definitely take my share of the blame. I felt like I aged five years between the All-Star Break and the end of the season. With each passing week I grew more tired and less focused. My game suffered, and our team suffered.

In the first round we beat the Minnesota Timberwolves, but it was a much tougher series than expected, extending the full five games before we advanced. That was not a good sign. In the Western Conference semifinals we played the Los Angeles Lakers, a much more formidable opponent led at the time by Shaq and a very young Kobe Bryant, but also such veteran stalwarts as Rick Fox, Derek Fisher, Eddie Jones, and Robert Horry. In short, a very strong and balanced team. We split the first two games at home before traveling to LA for games 3 and 4. I was struggling badly by this time, and not merely because of the wear and tear on my body from burning the candle at both ends. In fact, throughout the playoffs I had cut back on the partying because I knew that something wasn't right. But I still wasn't recovering.

We checked into the Ritz-Carlton in Marina del Rey two nights before game 3. Since we had practice scheduled for the next morning, I decided to lie low, and just order room service and watch a movie on television. I was flat on my back, remote in hand, when I heard a loud knock at the door. It was one of Gary Payton's boys, dispatched for the specific purpose of dragging me out of bed.

"G wants to know what you're doing tonight," he said.

"You're looking at it, bro. Just chillin'."

I shut the door, went back to watching TV, and figured

I'd be asleep soon. No chance. Another knock at the door. This time it was Gary.

"Come on, man, let's go."

"Nah, G, I'm just going to relax tonight. Seriously . . . I haven't been feeling right."

Gary gave me one of his dismissive looks, a disbelieving scowl that basically said, *You're full of shit.*

"Listen, V. You want to know why you're struggling? Because you're not doing what you were doing at the beginning of the year. You're trying to stay in the room, thinking about things too much. That's not the way we roll."

I'll give GP credit: he knew how to get under my skin.

"You're fucking with your routine," he added. "Never do that. Stick with what's working."

Nothing worked very well at that time, but there was a certain twisted logic to Gary's argument, and I quickly relented. In the end, I guess, the most important thing to me was maintaining Gary's respect and friendship, regardless of the cost. If my big brother truly believed we should be out at a strip club the night before practice—after we just got our butts kicked at home—then that's what we'd do.

"All right, G," I said. "Let's party."

Party we did, into the wee morning hours. I felt like crap the next day, and continued to play mediocre, uninspired basketball the remainder of the series. The Lakers took games 3 and 4, and then closed out the series by humbling us on our home floor by a score of 110–95. After winning game 1 we were swept four straight, losing by an average of nearly 17 points per game. Given that the Sonics had been to the finals each of the previous two years, and we were the number one seed this year, the exit was humbling, if not downright humiliating. I took it personally, as I was the new ingredient to this year's team. In the playoffs I had averaged 15.8 points per game. Respectable by ordinary standards, but a noticeable drop from my regular-season output. By the time we got bounced from the playoffs, that slippage had become at least a minor story: *What's wrong with Vin Baker?*

All the things that people had been saying about me my whole career—or at least that I felt they had been saying—resurfaced. *He's not a winner. He's not tough enough.* The sting of that criticism provoked a rise in anxiety, and that summer I began to self-medicate in earnest. It was an escape. As was the anonymous sex and the reckless spending. As long as I was drinking, I was a fun guy to be around. Everyone liked me. It was easy. And I was good at it. I was a generous drunk, buying for everyone, taking care of people whether they deserved it or not. I bought not just affection and friendship, but permission to behave inappropriately.

I spent most of that summer at home in Connecticut, where I split time between two girlfriends, each of whom wanted to believe I was faithful and monogamous, but was smart enough to suspect otherwise. One of these women I had known since my playing days at Hartford. The other, Shawnee Baker, I had met more recently. For years I would juggle these two relationships while being extremely promiscuous on the side as well. There were women in Seattle, women in Milwaukee, along with an endless parade of nameless, faceless women whose favor was curried at the end of long nights in strip clubs. How many partners? I couldn't begin to guess. And the weird thing is, I didn't even feel bad about it.

When I was young and rich and famous, and drinking myself blind three or four nights a week, I felt like I could do anything I wanted to do when it came to relationships; my narcissism knew no bounds. Shawnee would get at me, but we wouldn't really fight. You see, the money makes everything weird. It causes people to tolerate that which they ordinarily would find intolerable. When you're funneling ten thousand dollars a month to someone—more money than that person has ever seen before—accountability slips away. But the anger and resentment are there, simmering, waiting to erupt.

While squinting through an alcoholic haze, I managed to make everyone around me feel important: the women, the friends, the business associates, the teammates. Even at my worst, I was likable. On some level, I suppose, I knew that I was behaving badly—that I had drifted far from my Christian roots and the moral upbringing I had received from my parents—and the generosity was merely a way to compensate, a penance of sorts. But I was also a very good liar, capable of looking a woman in the eye and saying, "You are the most important person in the world to me," with such conviction and warmth that she had to believe it.

And then I'd say it to someone else the next day.

And someone else the day after that.

That's how I lived: not just from one drink to the next, but from one lie to the next. I believed my own bullshit, and the fact that others believed it kept me going. I honestly felt like I was a good guy. It's true that I was doing god-awful things, but I didn't feel like I was hurting anyone. Of course cheating and infidelity are hurtful, but I compensated by sharing everything that I had with the people around me: homes, vacations, cars, money. I enjoyed passing it around and seeing others smile.

Until the money dried up.

IN THE SUMMER OF 1998 I went to Cancún with Gary and a bunch of our friends to attend a jazz festival and hang out on the beach for a week or so. I did some drinking while we were there, but mainly I just picked up the tab for everyone else and hung out in my room, because I had begun to fall into a fairly deep depression. A couple of my buddies—guys who went way back with me and knew me to the core—understood the pain I was feeling, and I think they were legitimately concerned. But they also wanted to have fun; hell, we were in Cancún, right? Bottomless margaritas, sun and sand, crystal-blue water, and an endless parade of beautiful women. Mainly they just wanted me to keep paying for everything. Which I did, without complaint. It wasn't their fault that I had shit the bed during the playoffs. It wasn't their fault that I had become an alcoholic. That was on me. Every last bit of it.

One night Gary burst into my room and called me out. Like I said, Gary was a unique cat, unlike anyone else I have ever known. Not only could he drink all night and still play well the next day, he could put the game behind him five minutes after it had ended. Not that he didn't care—he did care, deeply. Gary was as competitive as anyone I've ever known when he stepped between the lines. But when the final buzzer sounded, that was it. Game over, time to move on. No sense fretting about it all night. After we got bounced by the Lakers, Gary was the first person out of the locker room. Showered, dressed, on his way, while many of us sat there in stunned disbelief. So he wasn't about to forgo a good time in Cancún just because the season hadn't ended with a championship. And he expected me to adopt the same attitude.

"Yo, V!" he shouted. "Enough of this bullshit! Pick yourself up, dawg."

I just looked at him and shook my head, which only made him dig in deeper. Trust me—when Gary wanted to hit you in the gut, he could do it, even to a friend. Maybe especially to a friend.

"Look at this nigga in here," he said, giving me that patented GP scowl. "Acting like he's Jordan or something."

It was exactly the right thing to say. The Cancún Jazz Festival was a major event that annually attracted huge crowds, including many famous athletes and entertainers. GP and I were hardly the only professional ballplayers in town, and the vast majority seemed to be having no problem putting the travails and triumphs of the previous season behind them. I took it all very personally, and very hard. I didn't want to leave my hotel room. I didn't want to face people who might ask what happened in the playoffs. Truth is, I was ashamed.

But Gary knew exactly which buttons to push, and insinuating that I was too big for my britches was the right one.

If all these other guys can go out and have a good time, then so can you.

WE WENT OUT TO A club and did our thing. I threw back some vodka and Hennessy (not at the same time, mind you) and started to feel a little better. Didn't get really hammered, just enough to soften the depressive fog that had enveloped me. On the way back to our suite, we passed the hotel pool. It was late and quiet, except for the presence of a single young woman. She was floating around, all by herself, minding her own business. She was also beautiful, which of course drew the drunken boys to her like flies to honey. They tried to talk with her, hit on her, compliment and otherwise charm her.

But she would have none of it. Barely even acknowledged their existence.

After watching my boys trip over themselves for a while, I finally intervened.

"Sweetie," I said. "Why are you being so rude? Can't you just say hello?"

I had no right to say this, of course. Part of me felt bad for my friends, but mainly I was suffering from a case of inflated ego. I was an NBA all-star—who was this woman to diss me and my boys? I was accustomed to just flashing a smile and a thick roll of cash, and having gorgeous women fall all over me. But not this girl. Uh-uh. Instead, she gave me a sideways glance, like she recognized me, and was sizing me up.

"You're Vin Baker, aren't you?" she said.

I nodded subtly, began to move closer. Here was my opening.

"Yeah, that's right."

She smiled; there was something mischievous in her demeanor, something that should have set me back on my heels. But I was too drunk and stupid to notice.

"You want an autograph or something?" I said. "Or maybe we can get to know each other better?"

She laughed. "Nah, that's okay. You're the one who came up tiny in the playoffs, right?"

The words caused me to stand and stiffen, and momentarily lose my breath. It was like she had hit me with a hammer. I mean, I know she was just sparring, and I know I had it coming, but it caught me totally off guard. Not only did she know who I was, but she knew exactly what kind of season I had, and how badly it had ended. And she knew that reminding me of this fact would quickly put me in my place.

"Damn, girl," I said. "That's cold."

She shrugged, laughed a little. The other guys went on up to the hotel suite, but I hung by the pool for a while, drawn to this woman for reasons I cannot quite explain. We ended up sitting by the pool for quite a while, talking deep into the night about music and basketball and life in general. We didn't drink. We didn't have sex or become intimate in any way. We just talked. Then we went to our respective rooms.

I never saw her again.

9

★ ★ ★

A FUNCTIONAL ALCOHOLIC

When you're an NBA all-star, accommodations are made and rules are bent, all in the name of money. I was a functional alcoholic in a world where that description shouldn't even be possible.

Drinking after games led to drinking on nights when we didn't have games, and sometimes during the daylight hours when we didn't have practice or games. Slowly I eroded, until I woke up one morning and discovered that I was an alcoholic, that all I really cared about was taking the next sip. It became less about having fun with my boys than about dulling the pain. The pain of withdrawal, hangovers, the pain of living. Fun was replaced by survival.

My statistical output during that first year in Seattle was

impressive, as was our performance during the regular season. But all of that was overshadowed by our early and unimpressive exit from the playoffs. This, in turn, led to even greater pressure the following year—there was a sense of urgency surrounding the Sonics during the off-season, a feeling that we would win a championship because, well, we had to win a championship. The time had come to stop making excuses.

That summer, however, brought a labor dispute and the third lockout in NBA history, which precipitated a shortened season and left the players with a lot of time on their hands. Rather than work out all summer in preparation for the new season, I drank. I figured the season would be canceled, I'd roll right into my free agent year and negotiate a new deal, and then I'd cut back on the drinking, get in shape, and nobody would be the wiser.

Early in the fall, the players staged an unofficial all-star game in Atlantic City, New Jersey, just to let fans know that we were still out there and ready to play ball. A lot of guys showed up for this event in less than prime condition. I remember seeing Shawn Kemp, for example, and marveling at his girth. The guy must have weighed 325 pounds.

"Whoa," I said to Gary Payton when we arrived at the arena. "Did you see Shawn? Man, he looks like hell."

GP just laughed. "Bro, have you looked in the mirror lately?"

I knew I was out of shape, but for some reason I didn't think anyone else would notice. I played like crap in that game, and had trouble even getting up and down the floor. But I was hardly the only person playing at half speed, so it was far from a wake-up call. In fact, the whole weekend was just an excuse to party. I had rented a limo to take me and some of the boys to Atlantic City from Connecticut. After the game, we went out and drank hard for several hours. The next morning we got up, showered, and crawled into the limo for a five-hour ride home. I poured my first drink roughly thirty miles into the trip.

What the hell, I figured. It wasn't like I had to report to work on Monday morning. The season was shot. Might as well have some fun.

Then an unexpected thing happened: cooler heads prevailed, management and labor reached an agreement, and the lockout came to an end. We were expected back in training camp in early December, and we'd be playing shortly after the holidays. To say that I was unprepared would be an understatement. By this point I was knocking back a fifth of Hennessy every day. Hennessy is a cognac, not as strong as whiskey, but in the amount I was consuming, it was strong enough to do a lot of damage. I showed up for an intense, short, preseason weighing nearly three hundred pounds, or roughly forty to fifty pounds over my playing weight. There was no way to hide it. I had a tendency to get heavy in the summer under the best of conditions, but this was different; this was liquor weight . . . thick, heavy calories that stick.

"How long will it take you to get in shape?" one of the assistant coaches asked me on the first day.

"Not long," I lied. "I'll be fine."

But I wasn't fine. I was an addict now, and I couldn't just throw a switch and reverse the erosion. Instead, it got worse. I kept drinking, every day, mostly by myself, and my performance predictably suffered. I was slow, unfit, and unfocused. Interestingly enough, my diminished state was most apparent not while trying to get up and down the floor, but at the free throw line, where I did not convert a single attempt in the first two games: 0-for-12. I was so bad that it quickly became a running joke, with fans in the arena standing up and applauding and cheering sarcastically when I'd go to the line. One night, a buddy—not a teammate—came up to me after a game and jokingly offered a suggestion.

"Hey, you ever think about"—here he paused and lifted his elbow and flicked his wrist toward his face, as if emptying an imaginary glass. "You know . . . before the game?"

"You're crazy," I said, laughing.

He shrugged. "You never know. Might help."

A couple of nights later, while drinking with the fellas, I decided to give it a test. I had a passkey with twenty-four-hour access to the Sonics' training facility, so I got into my car and drove over (drunk, of course). I hit the lights, grabbed a ball, and walked to the free throw line. Took a few dribbles, a deep breath . . .

Swish.

And then again.

Swish.

I must have hit 70 percent that night. While totally inebriated. In my addled condition, I started to rationalize.

I'm a free agent soon. I have to do something to turn this around. Maybe I really do play better drunk.

I was looking for any excuse to keep drinking, and to drink as much as possible. So I started drinking in the afternoon. Every day, including game days. Then I'd go out with GP and the boys after games, and then I'd wake up in the morning hungover, my body crying for relief, and I'd take a drink to cut the pain. And then another drink. Many mornings I'd drink an entire bottle of champagne before even getting out of bed. Pretty soon the drunk hours outnumbered the sober hours.

Remarkably enough, I didn't get caught. I'm sure some

people suspected—anyone who douses himself in cologne and keeps a stash of Altoids in his locker at all times is probably trying to mask something—but there was no intervention. One of my teammates, Olden Polynice, sort of called me out on the team bus, but he did so in a half-assed, benign way, walking by my seat and shouting, "What's that smell?" He knew I was drinking, and he wanted me to be aware of it, but he didn't want to confront me directly. Another time I almost got into a fight with Dale Ellis. It happened during a birthday party for Billy Owens, one of our teammates. The party was thrown by Billy's wife at their house, so it was a relatively quiet and subdued affair. Dale was a serious and competitive athlete who had no qualms about getting in the face of a teammate if he felt that person was not giving maximum effort. He had done this on numerous occasions in the locker room, and I had felt the sting of his words more than once. Ordinarily I didn't mind, because I had tremendous respect for Dale. He never slacked off, never did anything to compromise the team's chances of winning. A guy like that has earned the right to challenge his teammates once in a while. But the challenge should come within the privacy of the locker room, and on this night Dale called me out in public.

During a birthday party. For a teammate.

"You know, V . . . you gotta start bringing it every night, man. You can't just play when you feel like playing."

I bristled at the accusation. "Dale, I'm not sure what you're trying to prove tonight, but I'm not in the mood for it."

He scoffed. "Bro, I don't care what you're in the mood for. I'm telling you the truth."

It escalated from there, with the two of us in each other's faces, trading veiled threats and insults, until finally I asked him to step outside. The only reason we did not come to blows is because somewhere, deep inside, I knew that Dale's anger came from a place of love and friendship and concern. Yes, he was upset because I was not living up to my reputation as one of the best frontcourt players in the NBA. I had let my team down, and because of that we all suffered. Dale knew that I had a problem. He knew that my drinking had gone well beyond the stage of being a benign hobby. He was legitimately concerned about my health and well-being. I certainly wasn't willing to admit the depth of my problem, but on some level I understood what he was doing. So we hugged it out and went back to the party.

Another time I even got into it with Gary during a practice. He started talking trash, questioning my toughness. He had no idea what I was going through, the depths to which I had sunk. As much as Gary liked to go out at night, he would have found it inconceivable that anyone would drink before playing basketball. I was his little brother, and he was just trying to get me to play harder. It was, in his eyes, a very simple solution. Like most people around me, he was clueless as to the extent of my problem.

One person who wasn't clueless, but who said nothing, was Hersey Hawkins. I had the utmost respect for Hersey not only because he was a talented and dedicated athlete, but also because I knew he was a Christian. A part of me still felt strongly enough about my religious background that I was drawn to anyone leading a more moral and spiritual life than I was—even if proximity to that person sometimes made me feel ashamed.

We played a game in Chicago that winter, and during the trip I got caught by Hersey with my hand in the proverbial cookie jar. It happened at our hotel in the middle of the afternoon, a few hours before the game. I needed a fix to get ready for the game. Ordinarily I would have either brought something with me, or dispatched one of my boys to make a liquor store run. But I had forgotten to bring anything and I was alone on this trip. Additionally, it was freezing outside, so I wasn't about to leave the hotel. Instead, I called room service and asked them to send up a bottle of Courvoisier. Now, think about that. It's the middle of the afternoon, and I'm ordering an eighty-dollar bottle of Courvoisier—an after-dinner liqueur. Crazy, right? I mean, who wouldn't notice? It's not like I was anonymous. I was an NBA all-star who had a game that night. But I was willing to take the risk because I couldn't fathom the idea of playing sober. Not anymore. So, to deflect suspicion, I ordered eight glasses and a bucket of ice, and told the staff I was taking care of some friends. A short time later there was a knock at my door. Outside was a young man from the kitchen, pushing a table set up for a small party. Multiple glasses, a beautiful bottle of Courvoisier nestled in a bed of ice, rivulets of sweat glistening on its neck.

As I ushered the waiter into the room, a door opened across the hallway. It was Hersey's room. He had heard a noise outside and had poked his head out to investigate. For a brief moment, our eyes locked. He looked at me, then at the table, saw the bottle of Courvoisier, and just stared at it for a moment. Hersey knew full well that I was the only person in that room. He looked at me again. Didn't say a word. Didn't betray a single emotion. He just . . . stared. And I couldn't break his gaze. I was frozen, unsure of what to do. Should I lie and say I was expecting company? Should I just laugh it off? Should I apologize?

I'm sorry, Hersey. I'm an alcoholic and I need to drink before tonight's game or I'll play like shit.

Those words actually crossed my mind. Maybe this was the time to come clean . . . to ask for help. But instead, at first, I said only a single word: "Yeah." I don't know why I said that, or what it meant. A tacit admission of guilt, I suppose.

Yeah . . . you got me. Red-handed.

After a few seconds, I regained my composure and resorted to lying, a skill any addict learns to develop.

"Got a few of my boys in here with me, Hersey. They want to get your autograph later if that's cool."

Hersey said nothing, just nodded subtly. He looked away and retreated into his room. I followed the waiter into my room and closed the door behind me. Then I signed for the delivery and gave the man a nice tip to ensure discretion.

"Have a good evening, sir," he said with a smile.

"You, too." And I closed the door.

Did Hersey buy my explanation? I don't know. And after my first sip of Courvoisier, I didn't care.

Whatever Hersey may have thought at the time, or later, when my downfall became much more public, it's apparent now that he truly cared about me and loved me. Hersey is a man who doesn't just talk the talk, he walks the Christian walk. We never discussed that day in Chicago. Hersey never judged me, he simply prayed for me.

A FEW TIMES I HAD heart palpitations during practice or shoot-around, and this led to trips to the hospital and more cardiac exams, all of which revealed nothing. My body was crying out in protest over the way it was being treated, but I ignored the obvious warning signs.

My stats actually improved as the year went on, and I

finished with an average of 13.8 points per game. Thanks to injuries, though, I played only thirty-two games. There were no postseason honors, and I certainly hadn't looked like the all-star I had been in the past, but I'd performed just well enough to hold back the floodwaters.

Still, it was not a good year for the Sonics. Coach Karl had left prior to the start of the season to become the head coach of my old team, the Milwaukee Bucks. He was replaced by Paul Westphal, a former NBA all-star whose only head coaching experience had been with the Phoenix Suns, a position from which he had been fired two years earlier. As often happens, the coaching change instilled some new energy, and we got off to a fast start, winning our first six games. But we had holes on our roster and certain players who did not live up to expectations (yours truly chief among them), and quickly settled into a pattern of mediocrity. We lost six of our next nine games and finished the lockout-shortened season with a record of 25–25. For the first time in nearly a decade, the Sonics did not make the NBA playoffs.

After the season, I was a free agent, which meant I could offer my services to the highest bidder. My agent, Aaron Goodwin (who was also Gary Payton's agent), pushed hard on my behalf, dismissed any diminution in output as being the result of the lockout and insufficient time to prepare. It was an easy argument to make; lots of guys across the league came back out of shape and had comparatively mediocre years. My new contract, we argued, should be based on my full body of work, which included four appearances in the NBA All-Star Game and selection to the All-Rookie team, as well as the US Olympic team, for which I had recently been selected. I'd been in the league six years. I was twenty-eight years old. I was in my prime.

And I was a drunk.

That summer I did not make things easy for my agent. While he was negotiating with the Sonics, I was partying hard and heavy, leading to rumors that my behavior had gotten out of control. When the US national team traveled to Puerto Rico for the Tournament of the Americas, a pre-Olympic qualifying tournament, I was on a roster that included such superstars as Tim Duncan, Kevin Garnett, Jason Kidd, Tim Hardaway, and Gary Payton. It was an honor and a privilege to be part of this team, and to have a chance to represent the United States in Olympic competition. I believed that, and I felt it, and I tried to convey that sentiment to the media and to the coaching staff. There was, for example, a rather long and detailed story about me that appeared in the *Seattle Times* while we were in Puerto Rico. The story focused on the disappointment of the previous season, and my rather precipitous drop in production, and the measures I had taken to turn things around in the off-season. The writer cited several possible reasons for my disappointing season—injuries, lack of preparation because of the lockout— but generally went easy on me. There were veiled references to taking things more seriously and working hard and maintaining focus. A quote from Gary Payton offered only the subtlest hint of what might actually have happened.

"Right now, he's working out every day," GP told the reporter. "He can still go out and have fun, but he understands that he has to get up in the morning and work out, and that's what he's doing this summer."

He was right. I was working out. By the time we got to Puerto Rico I had shed more than twenty-five pounds of fat and gotten into decent playing shape. I was also drinking every day and hitting the clubs at night. Nothing had changed, except I was putting in more effort in the gym to offset the damage I was doing to my body when I wasn't in the gym. It was a hopeless fight, but one I had to engage in in order to protect the money I stood to make in free agency. A healthy player with my résumé was worth gold on the free agent market; a drunk, even with my résumé, was worth . . . well . . . nothing.

So I had to look good. I had to put in the work, even as I was destroying my body. I didn't even have the good sense to stay in the hotel and drink strictly in private while we were in Puerto Rico. I drank publicly and privately, which led to coach Larry Brown having to field questions from the media about my commitment. Larry was a basketball lifer who just wanted to get between the lines and teach the game he loved. He had no interest in discussing the late-night antics of his players—especially when those players were grown men.

"He's doing well," Larry said in that same *Seattle Times* story. "I think he wants to prove a point that last year was a fluke. So he's come in shape and he's playing hard. I'm proud of him."

Wally Walker, the Sonics' president, even called me that summer. The whispers had gained in volume, and he wanted to know if I was okay. I'm sure he was genuinely worried about my health, but there's also no question that his interest was fueled largely by business concerns. When you're in the middle of contract negotiations with a star player, and suddenly you hear that the player is not taking care of himself, you have an obligation to investigate. There are shareholders to appease, after all. There are season ticket holders and advertisers.

"I'm hearing some disturbing things," Wally said to me. "Are you okay?"

"It's nothing, Wally. Really. I've got it all under control. I'm getting back in shape and I'll be good as new next season."

I was drinking every day, more heavily than at any point in my life. I would never again be "good as new." And I knew it.

My agent wanted a multiyear deal—maximum value for the longest period of time. In essence, this was my career contract. Typically, this happens on the second or third contract, by the end of which your career will either be over or on the downslope. After all, the average length of an NBA career is less than five years. I'd been in the league six years; in four of those seasons I'd been an all-star. I was a proven commodity. It wasn't unreasonable to seek a guaranteed contract that would ensure financial security for the rest of my life.

Rumors notwithstanding, the Sonics wanted to re-sign me, but there was an understandable degree of apprehension surrounding the negotiations. My production had diminished the previous year and now there were rumors about my behavior off the court. Given these factors, it's not surprising that the team countered with an offer for a one-year contract. Basically, before agreeing to empty the bank vault, they wanted me to prove that I was fit and focused. I was represented by a talented and forceful agent who had no idea that his client was a full-blown alcoholic. Aaron rejected the offer and suggested to Wally that maybe we should look elsewhere for an employer who would like to acquire the services of one of the league's best frontcourt players. Wally blinked, and negotiations began anew.

In August 1999, the Sonics agreed to a seven-year deal worth $86.6 million. This made me the beneficiary of the most lucrative deal ever offered to an athlete from the state of Connecticut. Bigger than Ray Allen's deal. Bigger than Marcus Camby, Mo Vaughn, or Steve Young. Me—Vin Baker. The preacher's son from Old Saybrook. It was mind-boggling. I didn't feel bad about taking the money—it was further proof that I could abuse my body and still play professional basketball at the highest level.

I was invincible. I could get away with anything.

There was, however, just one little catch: I had to pass a very comprehensive physical examination. If something unusual was revealed through the physical, the contract would be nullified. This did not concern me as much as it should have. A thorough physical exam accompanies every new contract—it's a way for teams to protect their investment. All part of due diligence. I flew out to Seattle from Connecticut a couple of days before the signing, accompanied by my mother. Very briefly, during the days leading up to the deal, I had made a halfhearted attempt to cut back on the drinking. I still drank, but I prayed a bit, vowed to God that this deal represented not just a bullet dodged, but an opportunity to turn my life around. He had watched over me, given me a second chance when perhaps I did not deserve one. In return, I would be a different man.

But I didn't mean it.

The night before my physical, I got a call from one of my buddies.

"Let's go out and celebrate," he said.

"Nah, I'm in with the docs for a couple hours tomorrow. Gotta be good."

He pressed. "Nothing heavy, V. Just a couple drinks. You've earned it, bro."

Yeah, you're right. I've earned it.

We went out, had a couple of drinks, and that was it. I

didn't get drunk, didn't go overboard. The next morning I woke early, took a long shower, and went to my physical. Didn't drink that morning, either, because I wanted to be completely clean. But here's the problem: I hadn't anticipated that by the time I got to the doctor's office, I'd be dealing with some fairly serious withdrawal symptoms, the most disconcerting of which was an irregular heartbeat. My heart would race, then settle into a normal rhythm. Then it would race again. I could feel my pulse in my throat. I broke out in a cold sweat, the result of both withdrawal and nervousness. Waves of nausea washed over me. For a moment I thought I might throw up right there in the office. I could almost see my contract going up in smoke.

"Mr. Baker, are you all right?" one of the nurses asked.

"Yeah, I'm not sure what's going on. Maybe just a little nervous."

She smiled. "Let's try something different, and then we'll run the EKG again."

"Okay, thanks."

The nurse held up a hand, two fingers extended. "Take your two fingers, and press them right here"—she applied pressure to the back of her neck, near the base of her skull. "It has a calming effect."

I did as instructed, and almost instantly my heart began to slow. I pressed harder, moved my fingers around in a small circle, and the nausea receded.

"Pretty cool, huh?" she said.

"Yeah . . . thank you. That's much better."

If not for the kindness of that nurse, I might well have failed my physical. Her advice and compassion was worth $86.6 million. After a few minutes she administered the EKG once again, and this time the results were normal. As was every other aspect of my physical exam. I left the hospital and signed my contract that very day. The next night I went out to celebrate with my drinking buddy, GP. When he saw me, he burst out laughing.

"Damn! Somebody just gave this nigga eighty million dollars! You believe that shit?!"

And then we embraced. I was still Gary's little brother, and he remained, appropriately enough, the highest-paid player in the organization, but this contract narrowed the gap. We weren't equals yet, and we never would be, but we were closer than ever before. The funny thing is, I'm sure Gary felt like my troubles were over, like he had helped talk some sense into me. It was all so simple to him: Party when it's appropriate, take your work seriously. Don't let the two worlds collide. Mine had been crashing into each other for years; Gary just didn't know it. And the fact that I had just been handed the biggest payday of my life was not about to inspire a change in philosophy.

That's the difference between an alcoholic and someone who is merely a social drinker, or even a frequent and hard drinker. The alcoholic can't turn it off—the switch is broken.

I became a full-blown alcoholic during my time with the Sonics, and Gary was the person with whom I did most of my drinking, but I certainly don't hold him accountable for my failings. I take responsibility for my own actions. To the very end, I think he remained mystified that my problem became as severe as it did, or even that it was a problem at all. He didn't understand that drinking was my crutch.

A couple of days later, I went back to Connecticut and made an appearance at a summer league game, overdressed in an expensive designer suit and a ridiculous hat. It was a "look at me" moment. A chance to let everyone know that I was special, that I had money to burn. But no one said anything. I was still the hometown hero, and everyone seemed happy for me. A story appeared in the *Hartford Courant* about how hard I was working to get back in shape, proving I deserved the fat contract; this was in stark contrast to a column that appeared in the *Seattle Times* in which the writer basically accused me of stealing from the Sonics. The *Courant* story painted a picture of an all-star who had gone soft in his contract year, a good guy who had perhaps allowed himself to get too far out of shape during the lockout, but who remained one of the league's best players and a fundamentally decent person.

The preacher's kid.

I got away with a lot because of my reputation, because I was in fact a moral human being, albeit one who had clearly lost his way. The ink on my contract was barely dry when I started giving away money—not only to friends and family members, but to various charitable entities as well. I liked being thought of as a generous man, as someone who would never forget his roots and his Christian upbringing. That I was living an entirely different life from the one I shared with the public was almost beside the point. This was my way of atoning. I'd gotten away with an $86 million heist. I had to do something to make up for it.

10

★ ★ ★

A FRACTURED LIFE

The official diagnosis was "depression." That was the consensus among several counselors and doctors I saw in the summer and fall of 1999, consultations mandated by the Sonics (Wally Walker in particular) to ensure that the team was making a wise investment. The heart palpitations and anxiety attacks were actually a direct result of my heavy drinking, but both are also symptomatic of depression, so it was easy to reach for that diagnosis. Honestly, though? I wasn't depressed. I was strip-clubbing and drinking. The only time I got depressed was when I got caught. But I was perfectly happy to agree that I was depressed if it would deflect attention away from the real problem.

Not that the therapy sessions weren't painful. They were—

excruciatingly so, at times. But not for the reasons you might expect. I would admit to being sad, and to having feelings of inadequacy and fear, but I couldn't reveal the truth. I'd just taken more than $86 million from my employer. If I admitted to being an alcoholic, I risked all of that. So I would sit there on the therapist's couch, the tears streaming down my cheeks—honest tears, real tears—but unable to reveal why I was crying.

It was horrible, and it actually made me feel worse. I was enduring the agony of therapy, without the soul-baring catharsis that makes it all worthwhile. In short, it made me even sicker because the entire process was built on a foundation of lies.

Remarkably, given the amount I was drinking, I played pretty well that year. I wasn't an all-star, but I was still the second-leading scorer on the team (16.6 points per game) and the second-leading rebounder (7.7 per game). Admittedly, neither of those numbers is sufficient for someone who has just signed a contract worth more than $12 million per year.

With the increase in salary came a commensurate increase in scrutiny—not merely from coaches and management, but from fans and the media, and even teammates. When you sign a big contract, it's only natural for everyone to wonder whether you'll still be motivated. I'd be lying if I said I felt the same hunger to succeed that I had felt prior to getting the deal. Additionally, I let my guard down and stopped worrying quite so much about the possibility of getting caught. I became a bit more reckless while indulging my addiction, and predictably the addiction grew worse.

Vernon Maxwell, a shooting guard who came to Seattle in the summer of 1999 after eleven seasons in the league— long enough to have seen just about everything—was quick to call me on my bullshit. Vern was hardly puritanical in his outlook—he enjoyed smoking weed—but like Gary Payton, he believed there were lines you did not cross. When I would show up at practice, alcohol oozing from my pores, I was crossing a line, and Vernon would let me know it.

"Vin, gotta tell you. You're leaking right now, man."

"What are you talking about?"

Then Vern would scrunch up his face and sniff at the air. "You're leaking. I can smell it coming off you."

This wasn't something that happened once or twice. It was a regular occurrence in practice. I didn't even care. I would just ignore Vern and go right on playing.

Off the court, I behaved not just hedonistically, but gluttonously. In addition to sneaking alcohol on my own before games, I partied with teammates and friends alike throughout the year, only to an even greater extent than in the past. Strip clubs, gambling excursions to Vegas, dalliances with countless nameless, faceless women—all the things I had been doing in the past, only to a greater extent. The money did nothing to change me as a person; it merely intensified the worst aspects of the person I had become.

My first child was born in the spring of 1999. His mother, Shawnee, is now my wife and life partner, and Vin Jr. is my friend as well as my son, a fine young man—honors student and budding basketball star whose AAU team I have coached. When Vin was born I was splitting time between homes I had purchased for Shawnee and my college girlfriend, Mora, along with my place in Seattle. Work gave me an excuse to travel, and to be vague about my whereabouts, and money bought tolerance, if not acceptance, from those around me. Until the kids came along, it wasn't that difficult to be slippery and deceptive. Kids change things, obviously. It's one thing to be an absentee boyfriend with a thriving career; it's quite another to be an absentee dad. There are different expectations from your partner. Suddenly, you're supposed to be around a little more; you're supposed to *want* to be around.

Following Vin's arrival, I remember one night when I was at Mora's place, and she found out that I had become a father. She did not even know about Shawnee, although I'm sure she suspected. On this night, though, all secrets were revealed, and it wasn't pretty. I walked out of the bathroom and into our bedroom, and there was Mora, standing in the middle of the room, tears in her eyes. In her hand was a card, one I recognized immediately. Shawnee had given it to me right after Vin was born. It was a tender and loving card, the kind couples share with each other when they celebrate an important and moving event. You can imagine the details, and how they must have pierced Mora's heart as she read the words.

"I'm sorry, baby," I said. And while this was on some level true, it was far from an adequate explanation. I was sorry that I had hurt Mora. I was sorry that I had cheated and lied. Most of all, I was sorry that I got caught. I was not sorry about Vin Jr. being born. And I was not sorry about my relationship with Shawnee, for I loved her, too. I was in love with two women, and I was faithful to neither. I was a raging alcoholic and narcissist who felt like he could get away with anything. Beyond that, I thought of myself as a nice guy, and once involved in this love triangle, I didn't know how to get out.

"I was going to tell you," I said to Mora. This was another lie. I had no intention of saying anything until I was cornered. "I'm sorry you found out like this. I didn't want anyone to get hurt."

Several hours of tortured interaction followed: yelling, name-calling, threatening. To the extent that it was possible,

I convinced Mora that my relationship with Shawnee was over, or soon would be, but that things were going to be complicated because now we had a child together. In reality, I had no intention of ending my relationship with Shawnee, or with Mora. Within another year, Mora and I would have the first of two children, a boy named Gavin, and that left me with two families in two different places, and the freedom to visit both women under the guise of simply wanting to be part of my kids' lives. Both women felt they were the primary person in my life—or talked themselves into this anyway, against all logic and reason. But I was faithful to no one but myself. And so it went for the better part of a decade, until there were five children: three with Shawnee and two with Mora. I took good financial care of everyone involved.

I actually had people tell me I was being a responsible father, not just by funneling lots of cash to Shawnee and Mora, but by making a point of being involved in the lives of my children. I spent time with them. I hugged them and held them and put them to bed. Did it really matter that I was usually drunk when I did this? The addict lives from one rationalization to another. I was a good and responsible dad, writing checks of at least ten to fifteen thousand dollars a month to both Shawnee and Mora. As a fringe benefit, I was allowed to maintain sexual relationships with the kids' mothers. And of course the debauchery outside these relationships continued unabated: gambling, drinking, sex. I did whatever I wanted, and still I managed to cling to the reputation of being a swell guy.

IN THE FALL OF 2000, the Sonics' coach, Paul Westphal, confronted me on my behavior. Paul was a good man, a good Christian, a good coach, but he was under a lot of pressure. We had barely been a .500 team the year before, and if Paul was to save his job he needed to get the house in order and turn the Sonics back into a championship contender.

Paul was around me every day, and I would imagine he could smell the booze wafting out of my pores; certainly he noticed that my skill and effort had both diminished. Paul did not come right out and accuse me of being drunk during games or practice. Instead, he started riding me, day in and day out. And then, finally, one day he kicked me out of practice. Gary Payton did his big brother thing, tried to intervene, but Coach Westphal was undeterred.

"No! That's it!" Coach shouted. "He's out!"

This was Paul's way of sending a message to me and the entire team: *It's going to be me or you, and I'm lighting the fuse that it's going to be you. Right now.*

Indignant, I marched into the locker room, picked up the house phone, and called Wally Walker. I had no business complaining about anything. I was a drunk. I wasn't slurring my words or failing to show up for work. I just wasn't doing my job very well. Moreover, I was in a protective bubble. I was a max-contract player. I was GP's boy. Hell, I was making eighty million dollars! You're going to kick me out of practice? No way.

"Listen, Wally." I said. "I don't know what's going on here. I'm working hard, doing my best, and some people seem to have a problem with me." Now, this was simply not true. I was dead wrong. But that didn't stop me. "I don't know what Paul's deal is, but for him to kick me out of practice, it's just not right. You need to do something."

The next day when I arrived at the arena, I ran into Nate

McMillan, a former Seattle player who had recently become an assistant coach. He had a dour look on his face.

"They let Paul go," he explained. "He's in the locker room right now, getting ready to address the team. I know you don't want to hear anything he has to say, and he probably doesn't want to see you, so why don't you just chill out here for a while."

We were 6–9 at the time, not exactly tearing up the Western Conference. It's possible that Paul might have been dismissed regardless of my phone call to Wally, but I have to believe that by drawing a line in the sand, I hastened Paul's departure. The NBA is a players' league, and I wasn't the first star to have a tantrum rewarded with the firing of his coach.

Nate McMillan took over for Paul Westphal, and while Nate did a perfectly adequate job, he had his hands full. He inherited a team with high expectations and some significant problems related to salary cap (we had added Patrick Ewing at a cost of roughly $12 million per year), performance, and team chemistry. It was during the 2000–01 season that my productivity began to slide precipitously. I missed six games, started in only 27 of 76, and averaged just 12.2 points and 5.7 rebounds per game, easily the worst numbers of my career. It's one thing for a rookie or a modestly paid veteran to come off the bench and contribute in this fashion, but when you're in the second year of a long-term deal worth $86 million? People naturally questioned whether I had deserved such an enormous contract. It didn't help matters that the Sonics finished with a 44–38 record, good enough for only fifth place in the Pacific Division. We did not even qualify for the playoffs.

That summer brought a change in leadership to the Sonics, with Starbucks CEO Howard Schultz taking over as majority owner. I didn't know a lot about Howard. What I knew amounted to what I had read in the newspapers and heard from teammates. Howard was an exceptional business-man who had turned the Seattle-based Starbucks chain into one of the most successful retail operations on the planet. I had no idea whether he knew anything about basketball—on or off the court. And, frankly, I didn't care. When Howard told reporters very early in his tenure that he was not averse to making major changes within the Sonics, I figured it was just typical owner-speak. Whenever a team has a bad year or two, there is talk of a shake-up. But Howard was more detailed in his assessment. He pointed out correctly that the Sonics were carrying some extraordinary salary weight and not necessarily getting a good return on their investment. Under the circumstances, he said, every person on the roster would be evaluated, and no one was trade-proof, including Gary Payton and me.

That summer I met with Howard in Seattle. He must have known that something was wrong. Typically, when there is a change in ownership or front office management, or even in the coaching ranks, star players are granted an audience. This was different. First of all, Howard invited my parents out to his home as well—flew the whole family out to discuss my future with the Sonics and how the relationship could be mutually beneficial.

"Could" being the operative word.

"Vinnie, you need to make some changes," Howard said in that meeting. Although he didn't specifically accuse me of being an alcoholic, he did point out that I was not only com-ing off a terrible season—one in which I barely resembled the all-star I had been—but that I appeared unfit. The Sonics were paying superstar money for a guy who was no longer even a starter. This, Howard pointed out, was bad business. Howard was not a bad businessman, so he took this personally. I offered very little in the way of self-defense. I was a bloated 285 pounds. I looked like hell. The best I could do was capitulate.

"I know, Mr. Schultz. You're right. Next year will be better. I promise."

11

★ ★ ★

BACK TO NEW ENGLAND

It was bad enough that I was drinking before games. But when I started drinking *during* games . . . well, that's a whole different level of dysfunction. Inevitable, perhaps, given the trajectory of my disease, but still rather startling when I look back on it.

My in-game beverage of choice was Bacardi Limón, a clear mixture of rum and citrus flavoring that I would pour into a water bottle and store in my locker. Bacardi was crystal clear, so I could walk around sipping from the bottle without drawing attention. I thought no one would be the wiser; however, it attracted attention and suspicion long before I realized it.

I tried to be surreptitious: take a little hit in the locker room before the warm-up, then come back in before the game and take a few more sips, enough to keep the buzz going, and to allow me to play without nervousness, but more important, to stave off the effects of withdrawal. For the first few games of the season, that was the routine, but before long I was running into the locker room during time-outs and breaks between quarters.

"Excuse me," I'd say. "Be right back."

If anyone looked at me quizzically, I'd offer a follow-up explanation.

"Sorry, got to use the bathroom. Must be something I ate."

Then I'd take a few swigs from the bottle, throw in some breath mints, and return to the sideline.

It's not unheard of for a player to leave the bench during a game to use the bathroom, but I was leaving multiple times each night, and for some reason it never dawned on me that this behavior was viewed suspiciously by my teammates, coaches, the front office, and probably even a significant percentage of fans in the arena. I was blinded by a combination of addiction and arrogance.

On November 30, 2001, we played the Lakers at KeyArena in Seattle. Got our doors blown off, which unfortunately was not unusual at that point in the season (we were 4–6 through the first ten games). I played all right, had 13 points and nine rebounds in thirty minutes of playing time. Not exactly all-star numbers, but I had long since stopped striving for greatness, anyway; I was perfectly content to be merely productive enough to keep everyone off my back. What I didn't realize, though, is that once you are an all-star—once you sign the big contract and take the money that comes with it—the scrutiny never goes away. You aren't allowed to be pedestrian.

Coaches and newspaper columnists sometimes explained my downfall as "a lack of professionalism." It was such a vague and euphemistic phrase, one that didn't come close to capturing the severity of my problem.

The morning after the loss to the Lakers, I got a phone call from Wally Walker. I could count on one hand the number of times I had received a call from Wally; he was the kind of executive who would wait until he had an opportunity to see you in person. A former player, Wally was usually a pretty friendly guy. He was one of the more successful executives in the NBA. He knew how to run a team, and he knew how to evaluate and acquire talent without breaking the bank. But by now the Sonics' recent run of disappointing seasons was putting a strain on everyone in the organization. As soon as I answered the phone, I knew something was up.

"Hi, Vin, it's Wally," he said. "Listen, we have an issue that we have to discuss. Right away."

My heart began to race. I had trouble breathing. I paused, swallowed, and tried to feign ignorance.

"What's up, Wally? You're making me nervous."

I could hear him sigh on the other end of the line. "We know about the water bottle, Vin. And we need to deal with it."

All the years of lying and sneaking around had caught up with me, and what I felt more than anything else as I pressed the phone to my ear and tried not to cry was shame. Very quickly, though, my thoughts turned to self-preservation. What would happen to my contract? What would happen to my career, my livelihood?

"Wally, I don't know what to say. This is crazy. I mean—"

He cut me off immediately. Wally was in full executive mode. There was no sympathy in his voice, no compassion. He felt like he'd been duped. And now he was protecting his own job, for which I didn't fault him in the least.

"Vin, please. Just stop. We know all about it, we have the water bottle, and we're going to deal with it as an organization. There's no debate. Howard is out of the country right now, but he's going to sit down with you as soon as he gets back."

I said nothing in response, just let the conversation hang. I was stunned.

"Vin, did you hear me?"

"Yeah, Wally. I understand."

"Okay. And, Vin?"

"Yes?"

"We still expect you at practice today. Nothing changes until you talk with Howard."

For more than a week, life went on as usual. Basketball went on. The drinking went on. I stopped bringing alcohol to practice or games, but I continued to start each day with a bottle of champagne, and I drank Bacardi every night before I played. It wasn't just a matter of not wanting to stop; I couldn't stop. I was hopelessly and physically addicted. Even as the noose tightened around my neck, with the entire organization watching and waiting, I did my thing. Incredibly and inexplicably enough, I played pretty well in the first game after my conversation with Wally: 19 points and seven rebounds in a 14-point win over the Milwaukee Bucks. Two nights later I had 13 and six in a loss to the Timberwolves, the beginning of a five-game losing streak. I had six points in one game, five in another. In addition to being physically unprepared for the rigors of professional basketball, my head was completely out of the game. All I could think about was my impending meeting with Howard. I would be outed as not just an alcoholic, but also a fraud and a cheat. I would be fired and publicly humiliated.

There was no way around it.

As it turned out, nearly two weeks passed before Howard returned and I made another trip out to his estate. This time I was alone. No Mom and Dad, no teammates or friends. I remember downing a couple of shots of Bacardi before I left, just to calm my nerves, and then settling in behind the wheel of my car.

Howard is unique in the way he conducts business, and especially in the way he interacts with other people. Here is a billionaire who manages to project a bit of naïveté; somehow he always appears to be the underdog, even though he really isn't. But I think he identifies with the underdog, and maybe that's why he connected with me. As I rang the doorbell, I anticipated a swift and unemotional execution. After all, only a few months had passed since the last time I had visited Howard . . . since I had stood in front of him and vowed to change.

"Vinnie, how are you?" he said, giving me a big hug.

"I'm fine, Howard. Thank you for inviting me."

"Of course, of course. Come in. Relax. You're probably hungry, right?"

"Um, sure," I said, which was not true. Already I was completely off my game.

For the better part of two hours we watched a football game, had some food, and made sports-related small talk. There was no mention of the water bottle, no mention of my conversation with Wally, or of anything else related to my problem, and the Sonics' problem with me. Finally, Howard said he was tired and going to get ready for bed. He thanked me for coming, said he really enjoyed the evening, and showed me to the door. I was completely disoriented and confused. Had I dodged a bullet? Was Howard actually playing with me? Did he take some perverse pleasure in watching me squirm?

As we walked to the door, Howard suddenly stopped, as if something had crossed his mind.

"Come in here for a second, Vinnie," he said, gesturing toward a door that led to his office. I followed him in and we both sat down. Howard rubbed his chin, looked around the room for a moment, and then slowly began to speak.

Uh-oh . . . here it comes.

"You know, Vinnie," he began, "we all have issues. I have issues. My children have issues. You know what we do? We help them work through it in a positive manner. We make sure they know we love them, and that we're there to support them."

He paused, looked at me. "You see what I'm saying, Vinnie?"

"I think so, Howard."

"Good, good. You're going to be fine, too. And we're going to support you. I want you to know that."

"Thank you, sir. I appreciate that."

We got up, walked out of Howard's office, and shook hands at the front door, and I got back into my car and drove away, mystified by everything about the evening. First thing I did when I got home was pour another drink and sit in front of the TV, and try to figure out what had just happened. There is no question in my mind that Howard is a person who believes in the fundamental goodness of his fellow man, and who embraces the notion that everyone deserves a second (or third, or even fourth) chance. Howard and I had a rapport that is unusual for an owner and player. I liked him, and I think he liked me.

Business matters likely played at least some role in the Sonics' delicate handling of my situation. As long as I was still wearing a Seattle uniform and performing at least modestly on the court, I was worth something. The Sonics had invested $87 million in me, and while it was clear by now that they had overpaid, there was still a chance to recoup something on the investment. The Sonics could have gone after my contract based on my being unfit to play, but instead, they took the high road. They urged me to clean up while attempting to shop my services to another team.

Practically speaking, it made sense. I was averaging close to 17 points per game, and thanks to an assortment of diet pills, I had shed much of the excess weight that I'd carried over the summer. I had the appearance of an athlete, one who might still have a few good years left.

They could have blown me up, no question about it. They had every right to do it. But business and compassion got in the way. Howard liked me. He still likes me, but our relationship today is much deeper. He likes me enough now—maybe "love" would be a more appropriate word—to call me on my bullshit, and to demand more in return for his favors. Back then I think he just found it hard to believe that my problem was as severe as it was.

I got a call from Wally a few weeks before the All-Star Break. He left a message on my voice mail, asking me to call him back, which basically had me crapping my pants. I was

certain that the Sonics had changed their minds and were going to hammer me about my drinking. Instead, when I called
Wally back, he was friendly and encouraging.

"Listen, Vin," he said. "You need a big one out there tonight."

"I'll do my best, Wally."

"No, you don't understand," he added. "Rosters for the
All-Star Game are closing soon. If you play well tonight, I've
got a chance to get you on the team."

This was stunning to me. Wally had become something
of a cheerleader. I'd been playing all right, but not at the level
of an all-star. It just goes to show you how quickly the narrative can change, and how easily it can be manipulated.

"Thank you, Wally," I said. "I'm ready."

Oddly enough, I was at peace. My dirty little secret had
been discovered, and to my great relief my employer had decided not to make it public. At that point the goal for all of
us was simple: get through the season without screwing up
too badly.

The Sonics finished the regular season with a mediocre
45–37 record, almost identical to the previous season. We did
manage to make the playoffs but were eliminated in the first
round by the San Antonio Spurs. I felt relief when the season
came to an end. I was drinking hard by that point, having
escalated from Bacardi Limón to Bacardi 151. I wasn't hiding
liquor in my water bottle anymore—that was too risky—so
I opted for a more potent beverage, the effects of which
would last longer when ingested as part of my pregame routine. Every morning began with a champagne breakfast. Not
the glamorous kind, either. I'm talking about waking with
a hangover and immediately dulling the effects by drinking
straight from a bottle of champagne. By noon I'd usually pol-

ished off the whole thing. A few hours before game time, I'd start on the 151, mixed with Coke or Sprite.

I have a vivid memory from the San Antonio playoff series. I was lined up on the foul lane while someone was shooting a free throw. Tim Duncan, the Spurs' center, was next to me, and as he leaned in to get ready to box me out for the rebound, I could see him pull back and shake his head vigorously, as if something had startled him. Then he gave me a look of utter disbelief. He must have smelled the liquor coming off my body. Tim is the consummate professional, one of the greatest frontcourt players in the history of the NBA. I'm sure he couldn't imagine playing at anything less than full strength.

He said nothing, of course. That's just the way Tim is. But he knew. And I knew. And it hurt.

We had a team meeting after the season, as well as individual exit meetings—these are standard operating procedure for most NBA teams. I didn't even bother to attend. Instead I just took off for Vegas with some buddies. When Howard found out that I had skipped out on the meetings, he was pretty upset. I had completely worn out my welcome in Seattle. I was a shell of the player the Sonics had acquired five years earlier. I was perpetually banged up because I wasn't physically prepared for the rigors of NBA competition. I wanted out of Seattle, and the Sonics were only too happy to accommodate that desire.

In early June I got calls from both my agent and the Sonics' front office letting me know that several teams were interested in acquiring my services, including the Boston Celtics. Now, I was a New England kid, so naturally I had grown up a Celtics fan. I'd gone to school in Hartford; I had been a camper at Kevin McHale's basketball camp on

Cape Cod. When I was at Hartford people used to compare me to Reggie Lewis, who had played at Northeastern (another North Atlantic Conference school) before starring for the Celtics. The idea of coming back home and playing in Boston Garden was almost enough to make me think that it was possible to resurrect my career. But trade talk is common in professional sports. Rumors are part of the landscape, and as often as not they are merely seeds planted by front office executives to generate interest and speculation. A couple of years earlier I had come close to being traded to the New York Knicks, which also would have been a thrill. I was from New England, but southern Connecticut is awfully close to New York, so I'd followed the Knicks a lot as a kid as well. My hope, feeble though it may have been, was that by moving closer to home, I'd have not only a fresh start but also the support of friends and family.

When the Celtics called and said they wanted to meet with me about a possible trade, I was excited. I drove up to Boston and met with coach Jim O'Brien and general manager Chris Wallace. It was a shockingly pleasant and informal meeting. Basically, Jim and Chris had three questions. The first question was, "Do you want to play for the Celtics?" That was easy. Of course I did, for a multitude of reasons.

"I would love nothing more than to become a member of the Boston Celtics," I said.

Secondly, they wanted to know if I still loved basketball, and still wanted to play. Apparently they had gotten the impression that my diminished output was related to a lack of motivation.

"Yes," I said. "I want to keep playing. I need a fresh start."

Finally, they wanted to know why the Sonics were willing to let me go. This was the toughest question, for it implied a certain level of displeasure on the part of my employer.

I feigned ignorance.

"I really don't know what they're thinking. I just know that at some point in everyone's career, you kind of run the course as far as where you are as a player and where you are with that team."

I thought that was a good answer.

"We've heard about your drinking," Chris said. "Is it true?"

Busted!

I sat there for a moment, trying to fight back the anxiety rising in my throat. I folded my hands in my lap, surreptitiously wiping away the clamminess. I shook my head, as much for dramatic effect as anything else. I wanted this trade in the worst way. I wanted out of Seattle. I wanted to come home. Most of all, I wanted to keep the remaining $50 million on my contract, which the Celtics would have to absorb if the trade went through. Once again, I looked my bosses straight in the eye, and I lied.

"I do not have a drinking problem," I said. "I like to have a drink once in a while, just like everyone else, but nothing out of the ordinary."

Jim said he had heard stories from coaches and players who said they had smelled alcohol on me during games and practices. I didn't miss a beat. I'd been down this road before and knew exactly how to deflect accusations. You see, here's the thing about confronting an addict: It's almost more uncomfortable and difficult for the person who is doing the confronting than it is for the addict himself. The addict is accustomed to lying, hurting, deceiving. It barely registers as wrongful behavior. But the accuser is not accustomed to these things, so he feels terrible about the confrontation. He wants to believe that the rumors are untrue. The Celtics wanted to believe that they were acquiring the Vin Baker of 1998. They wanted me to tell them that everything was okay.

And that's what I did.

"There have been a few times when I've stayed out too late and maybe smelled a little at practice the next morning." I paused and smiled. "You guys know the NBA life. Sometimes we live a little too hard. But I promise you—I do not have a drinking problem."

Not long after that, the meeting ended. We all shook hands and I got back into my car and drove home. For the next month talks between the two teams continued. Finally, in July, the Sonics and Celtics completed a five-player deal in which I went to the Celtics along with the guard Shammond Williams, in exchange for Kenny Anderson, a talented but volatile point guard, the center Vitaly Potapenko, and the guard Joseph Forte. The primary players in the deal were Kenny and me, even though we were both considered damaged goods. On the day the trade was announced, the Sonics' coach, Nate McMillan, sounded more relieved to be rid of me than he was excited about acquiring Kenny.

"I believe the marriage between Vin Baker and the Sonics really had problems," Nate said. "He had lost his confidence out on the floor and just couldn't get it back. We couldn't take another chance on bringing Vin back and having him not want to be here."

Harsh as those words may have been, they merely hinted at the extent to which my relationship with the Sonics had disintegrated. But this was the company line, and I was happy to adhere to it.

In New England, naturally, the narrative was far less bleak. The focus was on rebirth and redemption, and the fact that I was coming home. Acquiring a four-time all-star who had grown up in Old Saybrook and played college ball in Hartford . . . well, that had to be a good thing for the Boston Celtics, right?

12

★ ★ ★

CELTICS INTERVENTION

A paradox of my life at that time was that the more deeply I sunk into the muck of addiction, the harder I tried to compensate with public acts of kindness and generosity. I gave away money and support to various charitable causes. I wanted to be a good person; more important, I wanted others to think I was a good person.

Even as the drinking and lying escalated, I searched for some evidence that a piece of the preacher's kid remained. I could cheat on my girlfriends, ignore the children I had fathered (in all ways other than financial), lie to my coaches and teammates. No amount of alcohol could deaden the pain of self-loathing, but if I did something good, something undeniably benevolent, it offered a respite from the awfulness of my daily life. It could be something as simple as signing an autograph or posing for a picture with a fan. It could be paying for a dinner with a bunch of friends, or buying cars for family members and girlfriends, or toys for my kids. Each small act of generosity, no matter how hollow, made me feel a little better about myself.

In the summer of 2002, before I joined the Celtics, I spent a lot of time at home in New England. I was drunk pretty much 24/7, but I still made at least a halfhearted effort to present the image of a native son grateful to be returning home. My charitable foundation got involved in a number of events, the most publicized of which was a softball tournament at an athletic complex in Branford, Connecticut. There were teams from all over the state, and it basically felt like a giant party: games being played on multiple fields, live music, food vendors, plenty of beer on tap. All the proceeds went to charity, so I felt pretty good walking around the grounds that day, seeing so many people having fun, and hearing compliments about the good work that I was doing, and how nice it was to have me back in New England.

"Thank you," I'd say. "It's good to be home."

Then I'd walk to my car, grab a bottle of Bacardi 151, take a couple of hits while ducking behind the wheel, and return to the fields.

In the middle of the afternoon, while I walked through a hospitality tent, I heard someone talking loudly. His voice was animated, his speech riddled with profanity. This was a family-friendly event, so the language caught me off guard. Also, I did not recognize the voice. I looked around the tent and eventually spotted the source of the commotion. Our eyes locked, and he began calling me out.

"Vin Baker! I gotta talk to you."

Rather than walk away, which would have been the prudent thing to do, I slowly moved across the grass to the other side of the tent, where the man was waiting. As I got closer, his voice escalated and his movements became more exaggerated. No one knows a drunk quite as well as another drunk, and I recognized him immediately as a member of the brotherhood, which only made me angrier. The guy was an embarrassment. Was I like this? I had to wonder. But I also wanted him off the grounds as quickly as possible.

"What's up, man?" I asked. "You having a good time?"

He stumbled, spilled his drink, and waved a hand at me sarcastically.

"Don't come over here bullshitting," he said. "You're with the Celtics now."

This took me aback. Drunks are by nature volatile and unpredictable, if not downright impenetrable, but this guy hit a nerve.

"Look, bro," I said. "This is not the time or the space for this, okay. You're out of line. So why don't you just go on home."

He stiffened and opened his mouth in a look of exasperation.

"What the fuck, dude? It's a free country. I can say what I want to say. You want to be a Celtic, you'd better be ready to play for a change."

I took two steps toward him, until we were separated by only a few inches. He was a head shorter than me, drunk, and putting on a public display of stupidity. Protocol dictated that I walk away, but I was ready to knock the guy out; I just wanted him to shut the hell up.

I could feel my hands balling into fists as I tried to control my rage, and at that very moment, just as I reached the point of no return, the man disappeared from my view. He was swept away in a heartbeat by what felt like a wave of humanity. I saw him on the ground, struggling for his life as three of my buddies wrestled him into submission. If you've ever gotten into a confrontation with a drunk, you know that they are unfamiliar with the phrase "discretion is the better part of valor." The drunk quite literally feels no pain, and so this poor guy fought on, trying with every ounce of his being to overpower three relatively large and fit young men. They tackled him and he wiggled away. They tackled him again, and he kicked them and bit at them and threw punches as if his life depended on it. The fight eventually moved outside the tent, where a massive crowd gathered, including lots of families and people from my local church. It might have been funny if it hadn't been so horrifying. The guy simply would not surrender, and his persistence—along with a few well-directed kicks and punches—only served to further enrage my buddies. All of a sudden, someone jumped into the pile and covered the drunk with his own body, to protect him from further damage.

That person was my father.

"Stop it!" he yelled. "Enough!"

And just like that, the brawl came to an end. Like a pack of dogs in retreat before the alpha, my buddies moved away quickly, while my father helped the drunk to his feet. He dusted the man off, asked if he was okay, and then told him to get the hell out of there.

Not long afterward, there was the threat of a lawsuit. I wrote a check and the whole thing went away quietly, without anyone from the Celtics or the media finding out.

The Celtics were on me from day one, as they should have been. I went to a couple of preseason workouts in Boston—

nothing formal—just to show that I was with the program and eager to start a new life. These workouts were held before the official start of training camp and were thus optional. I wanted to demonstrate seriousness and professionalism—except that I was drunk when I showed up at the training facility. Not falling-down, puking-on-my-shoes drunk, but just inebriated in the way that was a part of my daily life. A maintenance level of intoxication. In Boston, I started drinking more. The Celtics got a whiff of my behavior—literally; I reeked of alcohol every time I started to sweat—and called my friend Jay, who worked for my foundation and also served as a personal adviser on a number of matters. Calling my friend instead of my agent was actually a reasonably smart and compassionate way to go about the process of early intervention.

The Celtics told Jay there were indications that I had been drinking before practice, and that they were worried I had a serious problem. Jay calmly told them that this sort of accusation and alarmist response was probably not the best way to start a relationship with their newly acquired superstar power forward. Give it some time, Jay said. Everything will be fine.

However, as part of my deal, the Celtics assigned a new member of the organization to live with me. His name was Mike Procopio, but he went by the nickname "Sweetchuck," supposedly because he bore a resemblance to the character with that name from the Police Academy films (he'd had the nickname since high school). Physically, Sweetchuck looked like the last person you'd expect to see in the employ of a professional basketball team. He was maybe five foot seven, and weighed about two hundred pounds. But the guy loved basketball and was completely devoted to the sport, having coached at the high school and club level before he joined the Celtics the same year that I came to Boston. Sweetchuck has since become something of a legend in NBA circles, working in player development for a number of teams (he's currently the director of player development for the Dallas Mavericks). Sweetchuck specializes in helping players improve their shooting form, body mechanics, and footwork, among other things. In 2002, when he came to work for the Celtics, Sweetchuck was basically a gofer brought in to do whatever was asked of him. One of his first assignments was to take care of me.

A Boston native, Sweetchuck was assigned the ostensible role of helping me become acclimated to a new team and a new city. In reality, his job was to keep an eye on me and to report back to the Celtics if he saw any behavior that seemed suspicious—like drinking in the middle of the afternoon.

When my agent found out about the Celtics assigning Sweetchuck to live with me, he was furious. But I really wasn't that worried about it. I had a big place, so it wasn't like Sweetchuck would be sleeping in my bedroom or following me into the bathroom. I had become quite adept at drinking sneakily, and Sweetchuck was basically a kid in his first NBA job; I figured it wouldn't be hard to pull the wool over his eyes. In fact, I kind of liked the idea. By consenting to this degree of oversight, I conveyed a positive message: *Do whatever you want. I have nothing to hide.*

Every morning I'd get up and drink. I'd be on one side of the door throwing back Bacardi in the afternoon, and Sweetchuck would be on the other side of the door. If I went out after games—and I did go out—Sweetchuck would be right there, keeping a running tally. But here's the thing: my public drinking was not excessive. If you followed me to a club or a restaurant, I'd be no more inebriated than the next guy. It was the drinking I did in private that did the most damage. And Sweetchuck never got even a glimpse of that. He had nothing to report.

Unfortunately, my performance on the basketball court was a dead giveaway that something was wrong. In the first twenty games of the season I scored in double figures only three times—each time, just barely (exactly 10 points)—and never had more than eight rebounds. I was playing less than twenty minutes per game—sometimes a lot less—and frequently I looked and felt lost on the floor. Part of this was due to the fact that I was not suited to the Celtics' style of play, and quickly became an afterthought in their offense. In Seattle, despite my drinking, the ball always seemed to find its way to me, and I had numerous opportunities to keep up the pretense of being a productive player. In Boston, I never had a chance. Coach O'Brien saw through me from the beginning and almost immediately lost faith in my ability to stay sober or to be a functional NBA basketball player.

There is no better sports town than Boston. Its fans are passionate, knowledgeable, loyal. Play hard and win championships and you will be treated like royalty. Play badly and lose, and you will feel the sting of disappointment and anger, both in the arena and in the media. This applies to all teams: the Red Sox, Bruins, Patriots, and Celtics. Anything less than excellence is unacceptable. Losing is treated like an illness that must be eradicated. And if you have the misfortune to be a player who is not living up to the standards of his contract, you are considered a primary pathogen. I was making more than $12 million a year, which made me not only the highest-paid player on the Celtics' payroll, but also among the top ten most well compensated players in the entire league. An extraordinary salary provokes extraordinary expectations; I was not coming close to meeting those expectations, so naturally I began to hear the boos in Boston Garden. I was one of the least productive players in the entire league, a point driven home in a feature story done by ESPN in the first half of the season. That sort of exposure did nothing to ingratiate me with Boston fans, or with the increasingly frustrated coaching staff.

There was no way to stop the loss of skill, or to hide the fog that enveloped my life because of excessive drinking. The Boston offense was not designed for a low-post player like me. The team's big guys were more mobile players, so everything ran through the high post. One of the reasons I'd been able to conceal my lack of conditioning in Seattle was that my role on the court was so narrowly defined: dump the ball inside, turn, and score. Here, in Boston, everything was much faster and more complicated and demanding: flash to the high post, call for the ball, turn and square up, look for the back door cut, set a screen. Move, move, move. Mentally and physically, I just couldn't keep up.

One day Coach O'Brien called me in. Like Coach Phelan at Hartford, O'Brien was a no-bullshit guy, only he had the added quality of being from Philadelphia, the no-bullshit capital of the world.

"Look, Vin," he began. "I'm not even going to ask. I'm just going to say it. I can smell liquor all over you. You need to do something about this."

At first I said nothing, just sat there stone faced and silent. I was stunned. Through all my years of drinking and deception, no one had ever confronted me directly. This wasn't even an accusation; this was a coach taking matters into his own hands, trying to put an end to all the lying and the self-destructive behavior in one sweeping, parental gesture.

He didn't want to talk about it. He didn't want to hear any excuses.

This ends right now, he seemed to be saying.

Silence hung between us, thick as the stale air in a locker room. I stared at the floor, then slowly raised my head, and as our eyes locked, I burst into tears. Not because I was ashamed at having been busted, or because I was worried about losing a ton of money, but just because I was so tired. I couldn't live the lie any longer; I was almost relieved that they knew, and that I didn't have to hide it. I was crying because I needed help, and I didn't know how to ask for it.

But here's the awful thing: even in that setting, in that most intimate and trusting and personal of moments, I lied. I admitted to drinking heavily, but I soft-pedaled the details.

Just going through a rough patch right now, Coach. I'm trying to get a handle on it. I'll be okay, really. Please, trust me.

I left the office that day without receiving any sort of ultimatum. I had escaped the hangman's noose once again. Or so I thought. In reality, Coach O'Brien was merely exercising another step in the process of due diligence. There had been a meeting before the season, followed by the assigning of Sweetchuck as my personal watchdog, and now this. I wasn't aware of it, but the wheels of separation had been set in motion. The NBA has an enormously strong and vigilant players' union, which makes it very difficult to fire a player without paying his contract. Extraordinary cause must be demonstrated and fully documented.

There were appointments with doctors and counselors. At one point an X-ray showed something suspicious on my liver; the doctor, on the team payroll, told me it was something typically associated with heavy drinking. I figured, okay, this is it: four or five years of alcoholism, and now it's catching up to me. I'm going to die. Instead, he gestured toward my chart and said, with a smile, "Of course, if you play better, this all goes away."

To me, that meant I needed more 151. *Apparently I'm not drinking enough.*

Inevitably, people started to catch on. Teammates would occasionally make comments about the way I smelled, or the amount of time I spent in the bathroom. Sometimes I'd keep Bacardi 151 in my locker, hidden in plain sight, in a Coke bottle. I didn't drink during games—that had become too risky—but I'd sip from the bottle before practice or games. On the road, after games, I'd keep a bottle in my bag, and as soon as I got on the team bus I'd go straight to the bathroom and take a couple of hits. I was so consumed by my addiction that it didn't even occur to me that others might find this behavior strange. Paul Pierce was just a young kid with the Celtics back then, and more than once he shook his head in disbelief when he saw me emerge from the bathroom.

"That's crazy, V," he'd say with a laugh. "Just crazy."

On Christmas Day the Celtics played an afternoon game against the Nets in New Jersey. There aren't a lot of matinees on the typical NBA schedule, but the few we had posed a problem for me. First of all, the day started early, which meant I was hungover. Second, I had to make sure I was properly fueled before going to the arena, so I started drinking the hard stuff earlier in the day than I normally did. On this particular day, I woke up feeling badly hungover, and immediately threw back about a half pint of 151. By the time I got to the arena I was not only drunk, but still hungover from the previous day of drinking. Simply put, I felt like crap. I plodded through warm-ups in a heavy haze. What I did not realize was just how unprepared I was for even a modest effort. I played a few minutes in the first half, and with each lumbering trip down the court I could feel my body protesting.

Eventually I came out of the game, took a seat on the bench, and almost immediately became overwhelmed by a rising tide of nausea. I tried lowering my head between my knees. No good. I tried sipping from a cup of water. Even worse. My body turned cold and clammy. My heart began to race. I suddenly realized that I had reached the point where sickness was inevitable. Horrified and embarrassed, and utterly incapacitated by nausea, I jumped out of my seat and wobbled away from the bench toward the locker room. A couple of guys on the team asked if I was okay, but for the most part my departure went unnoticed. Once clear of the bench I sprinted beneath the stands and down a hallway; the added effort triggered a reflex, and left me vomiting into my hands as I searched unsuccessfully for the nearest garbage can. I finished the job by dry heaving into a toilet in the quiet of an empty locker room, as the game went on outside.

"Sorry, must have the flu," I said when I got back to the bench. I'm not sure anyone believed me. I played eleven minutes. Had six points and no rebounds, in a 36-point loss to the Nets. Statistically, physically, emotionally, and spiritually, it was the worst game of my professional career.

A FEW WEEKS LATER I was confronted again, this time by Chris Wallace. He contacted my agent and my father, just to make sure that everyone was on the same page.

"You need to check into a facility and dry out," Chris said. "And you need to do it now."

A quiet, almost surreptitious mandatory stint in a rehab

facility over the All-Star Break accomplished almost nothing. I was supposed to stay for at least three days but walked out—against medical advice—after only a few hours. When I checked in, I told my limo driver to just park around the corner and wait; I wouldn't be long. True to my word, I was out the door after only a single meeting. I jumped in the limo and told the driver to take me home to Connecticut, to the mansion I had purchased in Durham. I cracked open a bottle of Bacardi and was drunk before we hit the interstate.

By failing to complete the program, I gave the Celtics leverage to impose drug and alcohol testing for the remainder of the season, if not for the duration of my time in Boston. Not just random testing or monthly testing; the team was going to test me every day—at least until we got back from our next road trip, which was two weeks long.

The outcome was entirely predictable. I didn't stop drinking; I *couldn't* stop drinking. I was physically addicted and needed alcohol to stay alive. Every test administered on that trip came up positive, despite my use of masking agents (diuretics and the like) to try to beat it. On February 28, 2003, I was suspended indefinitely. My season ended with an average of 5.2 points per game.

Less than one week later, on March 4, I checked into Silver Hill Hospital, an addiction treatment center in New Canaan, Connecticut. I went in "voluntarily," but really I went in reluctantly, forced by my employer to deal with an obvious problem or face the possibility of losing my career and my livelihood. I knew I had a problem; I knew I was an alcoholic. But I wasn't ready to accept the help I needed, or to acknowledge the depth of my addiction. Mainly I was just pissed and embarrassed at the situation in which I found myself. This is not uncommon among addicts: the layers of resistance are peeled away over time, until finally there is nothing left but accountability. Or death. (Sometimes, of course, death is the ultimate statement of accountability, a final reckoning, if you will.) I was still several years away from that point.

I stayed in my room for the first twenty-four hours, refusing to come out for meetings or meals. I accepted the meds to ease the pain of withdrawal, and after a while I grudgingly began taking part in my own treatment. I was there for three months, and the whole time I used the alias Mike Evans, a nod to the actor who was featured in several 1970s sitcoms. However, everyone at Silver Hill knew who I was, which weighed me down with pride and embarrassment. Every day, in a place, an environment, where you should be absolutely claiming your disease, I was "Mike Evans." Just lying.

In rehab, without the pressure of basketball, I felt no anxiety. Once relieved of the physical craving for alcohol that comes with addiction, I no longer wanted to drink. I had long since passed the point where it had any positive effect. Now that I had effectively been removed from circulation, and no longer had to worry about playing basketball, the anxiety melted away. For the first time, I began to see clearly that perhaps the thing I had always loved the most in life was also the thing that caused me the most pain.

13

★ ★ ★

A CAREER UNRAVELS

There is no such thing as a former alcoholic. Once you join the club, you are a member for life. At opposite ends of the room are the recovering alcoholic and the practicing alcoholic, and somewhere in the vast middle is the alcoholic who hasn't quite made up his mind.

That was me in the late summer of 2003.

After Silver Hill, I was sober and physically fit for the first time in several years. I was eager to play basketball again, to resurrect my career, and to put a new coat of paint on the facade of my fading reputation.

The story that appeared in the *Boston Globe* on September 11, 2003, began with these words:

When Vin Baker opened the door to his brick mansion late
Tuesday night, he looked different than he did six months
ago. He was clear-eyed and harder edged. Most noticeably,
the puffiness that followed his jawline was gone. He sounded
different, too; stronger and surer.

I had opened the door to my home—to readers and the
reporter—for two reasons: to establish rapport and to make
it clear that I held a certain station in life. Yes, I had a drinking problem; yes, I had failed to live up the standard of expectations that came with an $86 million contract. But look,
everyone! I'm still a nice guy! And I still live in a house as
big as a hotel. I'm doing just fine, thank you very much!

So why did it bother me so much that the headline above
the story read "Baker: I'm an Alcoholic"? I mean, this was the
absolute truth, and I acknowledged as much in the interview.
Why, then, was I so angry when the story appeared? Why
did I find myself sitting there at the kitchen table, reading the
Globe, cursing the reporter for not focusing on something
more positive—as if an alcoholic publicly claiming ownership of his disease and vowing to do better wasn't positive.
Of course it was. But I felt betrayed and humiliated, and the
reason was simple: I still hadn't come to terms with my addiction. I neither understood nor respected its power. It was
easy for me to use the words "I'm an alcoholic" when speaking with a reporter, but I didn't really believe it, and I sure as
hell didn't want to be perceived that way. I'm not sure what
I expected out of that story, but I was completely unprepared
for the response it provoked. An extraordinary degree of humility is required of the recovering alcoholic; I hadn't yet
reached that point.

Working in concert with league officials, the Celtics had

structured an arrangement designed not only to encourage
my sobriety, but also to ensure that a relapse would provide an exit strategy for the club, which understandably did
not want to be left holding the balance of an $86 million
contract on a player who couldn't stay sober. After rework-
ing my contract to a more manageable one-year deal, the
club still wanted me to meet with officials from the league's
drug counseling office at specific intervals. For a while there
would be daily drug and alcohol testing. Later it would become more random but still frequent. My response was anger
and indignation.

You don't trust me?
Well, no, as a matter of fact we don't.

The maintenance alone was exhausting. The league had
taken $1.4 million of my salary from the previous year and
held it in an account pending completion of a year in which I
met all the terms of my return. A single failed test or missed
meeting would result in a declaration of noncompliance and
forfeiture of the $1.4 million. It would also set the stage for
my outright release. I began looking for enemies and excuses.

They're setting me up to fail. I can't go a whole year without
drinking, and they know it. Why should I even bother?

The NBA and the Boston Celtics rightly had me on a
short leash, but any leash is only as strong as the person holding it. Three times that summer I met with two of the NBA's
drug counselors. The first couple of times we met, once in
Las Vegas and once in Miami, they just wanted to know how
I was doing and to make sure I understood the parameters of
my probation. The third time we met, at a hotel in Boston,
the conversation turned suddenly dark and strange.

"I'm doing great," I said, in what by now had become a comfortable refrain. "I'm sober, and I'm ready to play ball. I don't know what any of this means long term, but I feel like I'm in a better space than I've been in for the last six or seven years."

They nodded, smiled. "That's great, Vin. We're happy for you. Now here's what we're going to do next."

There was a long pause.

"You give each of us fifty grand, and we'll let you know when the tests are coming up. That way they won't be so . . . random."

Were they serious? They wanted me to bribe them in exchange for proprietary information about the league's drug testing protocol?

I looked at them, tried to gauge their intent. "You're kidding, right?" I'll be honest: as an alcoholic—and, by extension, a master of deceit—my first instinct was to leap at their offer, illicit as it might have been.

For a hundred grand I can beat the testing and drink as much as I want? And I'll get to keep my $1.4 million? Sign me up!

They said nothing, just shook their heads calmly.

"I need to think about this," I said. And that's the way we left it. I called one of my advisers, a man named Steve Singletary, an attorney in Chicago, and told him what had happened. Fortunately, Steve's moral compass was functioning well, and he quickly talked some sense into me. "We're not paying anybody a dime," he said. "You can do this on your own—the right way."

For the next couple of weeks I continued to work the program: preseason workouts, meetings, daily visits to the lab for drug and alcohol testing. This was a big part of my day, driving forty minutes each way to pee in a cup. But I was into it; I was motivated. In the eyes of the league, the most important part of compliance is a clean test. For an athlete trying to recover from a drug or alcohol violation, that's 99 percent of the battle. With each clean test, my confidence increased.

Then, one day, I got a call from Steve.

"Man, I've got some bad news for you."

I couldn't imagine what he was talking about. I was totally clean.

"What is it, Steve?"

"They're taking your $1.4 million."

I was stunned. "On what basis?"

Steve sighed. "They're saying you haven't stayed in touch with your counselors."

There was some truth to this. Following the meeting in Boston, and the solicitation of a bribe, I stayed clear of the two counselors. No money changed hands, and I figured that was the end of it. It honestly never occurred to me that by turning them down—by simply trying to play according to the rules—I'd made some sort of tactical error. Maybe they really expected me to pay them; maybe they were hoping I'd agree and then they could report me for attempted bribery. Either way, I'd been set up, and there was absolutely nothing I could do about it. What was I going to say? To whom would I report the solicitation? I was a drunk and a liar. Who would believe me? It was one of those moments in life where you see the train coming down the tracks, and there is nothing you can do to stop it. You either get out of the way or you get run over.

I was not strong enough to withstand the collision. The anger over being duped, and of forfeiting $1.4 million that I should not have lost, ate me up inside. After five months of sobriety—easily the longest such period of my adult life—I started feeling sorry for myself again, and pretty soon I felt the pull of alcohol. Ironically, I was actually fit and playing reasonably well, so much so that I sensed an almost unreasonable standard of hope and expectation on the part of the Celtics.

One day in practice Coach O'Brien set up a game of one-on-one between me and Antoine Walker. This was not common in NBA camps. Antoine was the Celtics' biggest star, having been in Boston his entire career after playing at the University of Kentucky. A six-foot-eight power forward, he was an impressively consistent and versatile player, averaging better than 20 points, eight rebounds, and four assists per game during his seven years in Boston. In contrast, I had been the picture of inconsistency. Why any of the coaches would want me to play a game of ones with Antoine just a couple of weeks into the preseason struck me as a mystery, and a slightly cruel one at that. Most teams avoid this type of exercise specifically because it can lead to hurt feelings and resentment, not to mention injuries. You don't get to the NBA without being hypercompetitive, and there is nothing that brings out this competitiveness quite like a game of one-on-one.

On a team overflowing with big personalities, Antoine was one of the biggest, in ways both positive and negative. His response, at first, was to wave a hand dismissively and tell Coach O'Brien, "Nah, I don't do ones, man. No way." But Jim pulled him aside and they talked for a few minutes, and the next thing you know the ball was rolled out and Antoine and I went at it. This had great potential to backfire. Antoine and I were not buddies who would simply bump against each other a little and take some outside jump shots until the game was settled. He was an established star on the Celtics and I was a former star trying to rebuild my career. And we played the same position. I'm sure Antoine thought he was a substantially better player than I was at that time; I thought he was somewhat overrated. So we played, didn't even keep score, just beat each other up and traded baskets for a while, until both of us were drenched with sweat. Then we shook hands and finished practice.

Under the circumstances, I felt like I had acquitted myself reasonably well, but that didn't lessen the shock a few days later when I got a call from Danny Ainge, the former Celtics star who recently had been hired as director of basketball operations. Danny would eventually become known for making bold personnel moves, and this was one of the first.

"We're moving Antoine," he told me.

Stunned almost to the point of speechlessness, I finally managed to spit out a single word.

"Why?"

The answer had less to do with any perceived deficiencies in Antoine's game than confidence in my ability to successfully reboot my career in Boston. Like, immediately.

"We just think you're ready," Danny explained. And that was that. Nine days before the start of the season, on October 21, 2003, the Celtics sent Antoine Walker—a player who had led the team in rebounds and assists, and was second in scoring the previous year—to the Dallas Mavericks as part of a five-player trade. This did not please most Celtics fans, or the media, which was skeptical that a guy fresh out of rehab could step in and replace a proven commodity like Antoine Walker. I questioned it myself. Sure, I was still relatively young and only a few seasons removed from being an all-star, and I was fitter than I'd been in years, but I knew in my heart that I had a long way to go, and that my grip on sobriety was tenuous at best.

From a purely basketball standpoint (at least on paper), it was a sound move by Ainge. The Celtics got Raef LaFrentz, technically a center but really a stretch power forward, along with a future first-round draft pick. Adding Raef would allow me to move into the post. But rather than feeling excitement over the possibilities created by this trade, I felt nothing so much as pressure. Instead of playing in Antoine's shadow, I'd be one of the focal points of the Celtics' offense, which scared the crap out of me. What if I failed? The Celtics had been a playoff team the previous year, and expectations were now even higher. If we didn't meet those expectations, I'd be held responsible. Not me alone, of course, but I saw it that that way. Almost as soon as the trade went through, I felt a surge of anxiety that never really went away.

Actually, the first anxiety attack occurred before Antoine even left, but after I had received word that the Celtics were shopping him. I knew the trade was imminent. One night before a preseason game in New Jersey, I found myself sitting alone in my hotel room, staring at an open minibar, contemplating the wondrous effects of that magic elixir known as alcohol.

Wouldn't take much, that's for sure. Been sober for five months— probably only need one or two of those little bottles to set me right, help me get in the proper frame of mind.

As luck would have it, there was a tiny bottle of Bacardi. I plucked it from the shelf, rolled it around in my hand for what must have been ten or fifteen minutes. Just sat there looking at it, fondling it, imagining how the contents would taste. For months I hadn't even desired a drink; now the craving was overwhelming. I closed my eyes and squeezed the bottle tight, tried to break it in the palm of my hand. I blinked back tears. And then, for some reason, I tossed the bottle into my gym bag.

Not now. Maybe later. At the arena.

I did not drink that night, but the seed of self-doubt had been planted. I carried that little bottle around with me for the next few days in a deliberate dance of temptation, although eventually I tossed it in the garbage. Roughly one week later Antoine was gone and the regular season was about to start, and I knew that I'd be getting significant minutes in his place. I had already rationalized self-medication as merely a means to an end: drinking would once again allow me to face the pressure of basketball. But I needed a less transparent means of achieving that goal. I remembered hearing once that many types of mouthwash contain alcohol. I started doing some research. It was true, of course: there is alcohol in mouthwash.

Crazy as it sounds, I figured I could get enough alcohol into my system by drinking mouthwash, without suffering the unwanted side effect of smelling like a distillery. That's how I wound up standing in the bathroom of my home in Boston, just an hour or so before practice, choking down about a half bottle of Listerine. It was one of the small bottles, maybe sixteen ounces, so I drank probably eight ounces of 50 proof—enough to give me a solid buzz, but not before causing my stomach to roar in protest. I leaned over the sink, prepared to vomit, but somehow managed to fight off the urge.

Easy . . . Easy . . .

After a minute or two, the nausea passed, replaced by a warm glow, the likes of which I hadn't felt in months. I felt no remorse, no sadness, no shame. Mainly I just felt . . . relief.

A predictable escalation followed, although not in the way

you might expect. I restricted my alcohol intake to Listerine, and naturally the amount required to get the job done increased dramatically. Before long I was drinking a full 1.5-liter bottle (or more) every day. My drinking was weird and pathetic and exercised in complete solitude. Sobriety seemed to be overrated, as I was playing better than I had in a couple of years—averaging more than 15 points and seven rebounds per game through the first two months. Coach O'Brien was so impressed and optimistic that he even said I was starting to look like an all-star again, and began mentioning that honor as a possibility. To me, this was validation.

See what happens when you drink, Vin? The game is so much easier.

Inevitably, I began failing some of the random tests. Contractually, I was permitted three strikes. The first two would results in suspensions, while a third would give the Celtics leverage to terminate my contract. There was a relatively quiet one-game suspension after the first positive test. News of the second positive came down while we were in Miami for a game against the Heat. At shootaround that morning I got a call from Danny Ainge, who had made the trip with the team.

"Let's go to a movie this afternoon," he said.

"A movie?"

"Yeah, just relax, then we can talk afterward."

"Okay, Danny. Whatever you say."

Danny is a compassionate guy and wanted to try to help me. There were two dirty tests now, he said. Maybe it was time to think about an exit strategy. I appreciated his sensitivity, but did nothing to change. In January the Celtics suspended me for ten games; there was another failed test, and in February my contract was terminated. I cleared waivers, but rather than try to catch on with another team, I decided to go back home and sit out the remainder of the season. My drinking had not yet escalated to its previous level, so I tried to convince myself that if I just took some time off and got back in shape and let some of the dust settle, I could start over again the following season.

My relapse this time had been highly public. I was now one of the more infamous drunks in the annals of basketball, if not all of professional sports. And yet, somehow, the NBA did not close its doors to me completely. Shortly after I got home I received a phone call from Larry Brown, who was at the time the head coach of the Detroit Pistons. Larry had also been the Olympic coach in 2000, the year I played for the US team. Larry is one of the game's most revered and nomadic coaches. He never stays in one place for long, but anyone who has had the opportunity to play for him knows that he has a great basketball mind. More important, he has a big heart. He legitimately cares about his players, both on and off the court. Coach Brown called several times, encouraging me to stay strong and to not give up on life or basketball.

Then I got a call from Pat Riley, who had just stepped down as coach of the Miami Heat, but who remained the team's general manager. Pat sent me a laminated poem of encouragement and inspiration, which totally blew me away. Like Coach Brown, he apparently looked past all the transgressions and squandered opportunities, and reached out to me at one of my lowest points. Then came calls from the Knicks, and from other teams, all offering me a chance to play again. Here I was, a relapsed alcoholic, on the verge of washing out of the league, and I had somehow become one of the most sought-after free agents on the market. (Not only that, but thanks to the NBA Players Association, I was able to salvage roughly half the value of what I was owed on my contract from the Celtics, which amounted to nearly $18 million.)

I was grateful, but I was also perplexed. It was like the whole world was willing to forgive me, and to enable me, simply because I was a basketball player, because I had a gift.

In April I was reinstated by the NBA, and what followed, inexplicably, was a bidding war for my services. I was still drinking Listerine every day, and I hadn't even been to rehab following my dismissal from the Celtics. I had a serious problem, and everyone knew it, and yet there I was, in Miami with my agent, negotiating with Pat Riley about joining the Heat for the remainder of the season. I was almost ready to accept the offer when the Knicks came at me again—hard. I had a great talk with Isaiah Thomas, who at the time was the team's president of basketball operations, and decided that I'd be better off playing in the Northeast, closer to home. And there was something incredibly appealing about playing in New York, at Madison Square Garden. That I was thoroughly unprepared for any of this was almost beside the point. I accepted the deal and sneaked out of the hotel without even telling the Heat or Pat Riley that I had chosen a different suitor.

A few hours later I was in Philadelphia, where the Knicks were playing the 76ers. This was March 12, 2004; I hadn't played a game in nearly two months. I was out of shape and struggling badly with my addiction. In fact, the first thing I did when I got to shootaround that afternoon—I went straight from the airport to the arena—was to suck down two or three little bottles of Listerine, which I always kept in my travel bag. I remember standing at my locker, listening to the sound of leather thumping against wood as the Knicks practiced just a few yards away. I drank quickly and urgently. Then I sat down and slowly put on my new practice uniform. I was anxious and scared; there was no way I was going to try to play sober.

That night I took a seat on the bench and waited to see whether I'd get a chance to play. When Tim Thomas got in foul trouble in the first half, I knew what was coming. Lenny Wilkens, the Knicks' coach, paced back and forth in front of the bench. Suddenly he stopped and looked at me.

"You play power forward, right?"

"Ummm. . . . yeah, Coach. I play power forward."

"All right, get in there."

I had two points and two rebounds in fourteen minutes of playing time. Didn't do anything special, but didn't embarrass myself, either. For a while I was part of the regular rotation, getting twenty minutes or more per game and playing pretty well, especially given that I was knocking back roughly one and a half large bottles of Listerine every day. By the time the playoffs rolled around, though, my time had diminished considerably. We got swept by the Nets in the first round, and I played only nine minutes in each of the first two games. In the final game, I played twenty-four minutes and had 12 points and six rebounds. A solid game. In fact, when I fouled out, as I was walking to the bench, I got a standing ovation from the Garden crowd. It caught me by surprise and provoked a flood of emotion, so much that by the time I got to the bench, tears were streaming down my cheeks.

Tim Thomas, with whom I had gotten close, stopped me as I tried to sit down.

"Man, don't let them see you like this," he said. "Be strong."

He didn't get it. He thought I was just upset about losing

or fouling out. Instead, I was upset that I hadn't played more in the series, and that I hadn't stayed sober to prove what I could do. I'd been dumped by the Celtics and given a new lease on life, and still I was medicating with alcohol. And despite all of that, God saw fit to give me a standing ovation in Madison Square Garden.

It was so much more than I deserved.

14

★ ★ ★

LOSING EVERYTHING

The downward spiral continued for several more years, with sustained periods of heavy drinking interrupted by brief and half-baked attempts at sobriety. Basketball ended well before the drinking. In three years—from 2003 through 2006—I played for four different teams: the Celtics, Knicks, Rockets, and Clippers. People kept giving me chances, but I'd let them down, or discover that too much had been lost. I tried to blame some of my problems on depression, but I never received a firm diagnosis. The depression was a by-product of alcoholism. I drank because of loneliness and anxiety, not depression.

I did another stint in rehab in 2005 after playing part of the season with the Rockets, and then stayed in Houston, working with John Lucas, a former NBA player, a recovering drug addict, and a counselor who has done terrific work with athletes over the years. John is a tough-love kind of guy who likes to get in your face and break down your defenses. I needed that.

"Who am I getting today?" John would shout when we'd get together. "Am I getting the old-ass Vin Baker . . . or the *old* Vin Baker?"

That was his mantra, and here's what it meant: Am I working with tired, old washed-up Vin Baker . . . or am I working with the guy who used to be an NBA all-star? John was loud, too, so when he'd say this kind of stuff, everyone could hear it. There was no escaping his wrath. Anyone who has ever worked with John knows that he does nothing halfway. He is fully committed to his job, and to helping the men with whom he works. It's not for everyone. God knows, it wouldn't have been for me when I was younger and more sensitive, but I was desperate enough now to take whatever John dished out, and to do my best to meet his high standards. I got stronger, fitter, and began to look like a professional ballplayer again. I wasn't drinking at all—not even Listerine. For the first time in more than two years, I was totally clean and sober.

That's when I discovered Xanax.

It was first prescribed to me in the fall of 2005 by a doctor in Rhode Island who determined—not unreasonably—that since my primary issue was anxiety, why not treat the anxiety in a professional and supervised manner? This is an old and heated argument in the fields of both addiction counseling and mental health. There is a school of thought that says many people become addicts while trying to self-medicate. Certainly this was true in my case. I smoked weed and drank alcohol primarily to ease the anxiety that I sometimes found to be crippling. But now, many years later, I wouldn't let my-self off the hook quite that easily. I also liked getting high and I liked getting drunk; for a long time it was fun. But when it became a crutch used primarily to help me play basketball in a more relaxed state, then it became an addiction, pure and simple. My doctor felt that if we used medication to alleviate the symptoms of my underlying anxiety, I would no longer feel the need to self-medicate with alcohol before playing basketball.

There was just one problem: Xanax, like its cousin Val-ium, is a highly addictive drug. Both are in the benzodiaz-epine family and are noted for providing fast and effective relief of symptoms related to all manner of anxiety and panic disorders. Simply put, Xanax works, which is why it used to be so commonly prescribed for patients struggling to cope with anxiety. Xanax is best (and safest) when used primar-ily for crisis relief, as opposed to daily maintenance. I was instructed to use it only "as needed," but of course I quickly decided that I needed it all the time.

The first time I took Xanax, I took only a single pill, as prescribed. I wanted to see how I would feel on it, and what effect it would have on my coordination and fitness, so I swallowed one pill at home, waited about a half hour, and then went out into my backyard, where I had a basket-ball court, to put up some shots. To be honest, I didn't feel much of anything. The Xanax hadn't made me groggy or disoriented, which was good, but neither had it made me feel any looser or different in any way. In other words, it seemed ineffective. But this was a controlled and stress-free environ-ment, so it was hard to tell. I took another pill just to see what would happen, and sure enough, I felt a warm sensation and an instantaneous feeling of relaxation.

Oh, yeah . . . this is great!

Prior to its being prescribed to me, I had never even heard of Xanax. I did not know how strong or addictive it was; I didn't even know that it was a controlled substance—a narcotic subject to some serious and stringent laws and penalties. I knew only that it gave me the same sort of buzz that I got from alcohol, only without all the unpleasant side effects. I could take a couple of Xanax and all my worries and anxiety would melt away. I could talk comfortably with anyone, and I could play basketball without feeling nervous. Best of all, no one had any idea what I was doing. There were no liquor bottles to hide, no smells to mask. I just flipped the cap on a tiny plastic container and shook out a couple of pills. I could do this literally anywhere without causing a disruption or inviting suspicion. Best of all, it was perfectly legal and socially acceptable. Hey, I had a prescription! I was under a doctor's care, for goodness' sake. I wasn't a drug addict; I was just taking my medication.

The only voice of reason in all of this was provided by John Lucas, who wasted no time in calling bullshit.

"A drug is a drug," he said when I told him I'd been prescribed Xanax for my anxiety. "Vin, you're an addict. You can't just trade one drug for another and not expect consequences."

John believed in total abstinence as the only means to freedom from addiction. I would always be an addict, he said; it was just a matter of whether I was an active addict or an addict in recovery.

Within a month's time I had become hopelessly hooked on Xanax. I wasn't drinking—no need to do that when you're gobbling thirty, forty, fifty pills a day. Which is what I was doing. At its zenith, my addiction required as many as eighty pills a day. Needless to say, I did not have a prescription to cover that volume of medication, so I had to find other, more creative ways to feed my habit. I developed a network of friendly physicians; I went underground and bought Xanax on the black market. As with any addiction, keeping the fire stoked became a full-time job.

I signed with the Clippers that winter and moved to Los Angeles, where the procuring of narcotics is something of an industry. I developed a network of contacts—friends, associates, doctors both reputable and shady, flat-out drug dealers. I learned to use my celebrity as a means to obtain prescriptions or refills. For example, sometimes I'd walk into a CVS, explain that I needed a new batch of Xanax, but didn't have time to get to my doctor. I would smile and politely explain the situation, try my best to act charming and not desperate, and remind the person behind the counter that I was a basketball player for the LA Clippers. More often than not, I was able to talk my way into a refill. If not, I'd try a different doctor. If that didn't work, I'd make a phone call. If you have money and status in LA, you can find drugs.

Xanax worked beautifully for me—it cut my anxiety down to practically nothing and did not inhibit my athletic performance nearly to the extent that alcohol did. Xanax, to me, was like a gift from heaven. Pop a few pills and instantly I felt the same sense of euphoria that I felt after guzzling a liter of Listerine, without any of the attendant queasiness or bloat. It was like I was taking a synthetic steroid: all the benefits with little risk of getting caught.

I was playing well in practice, too, although those performances did not translate into game time. For most of my tenure with the Clippers I was glued to the bench, in part because the team was playing well and there was no reason to mess with the rotation by the time I arrived, two-thirds of the way through the season. The thing is, I was killing it in practice. Seriously—we'd have these pickups games at the end of practice and I felt like a kid again. The coach, interestingly enough, was Mike Dunleavy, who had been my coach in Milwaukee when I first got into the league. Obviously there was some baggage there, but I don't think Mike held it against me. I think he believed he had a playoff team and saw no reason to risk that status by making room for an old alcoholic power forward who hadn't done much in the last few years. I tried to talk to him about playing time, but Mike did not give me reason to be optimistic.

With time on my hands and no great concern about getting meaningful minutes, I grew bored. Pretty soon, I began taking advantage of my new home's proximity to Las Vegas. I liked playing cards and had made plenty of trips to Vegas and Atlantic City in the past, but it wasn't until I moved to LA and developed a raging Xanax addiction that I became a compulsive and spectacularly ineffective gambler. I started making the trip to Vegas a couple of times a week—maybe more. It wasn't unusual for me to drop ten thousand dollars or more each time I went. I rarely won, and if I did, I ended up giving it back—and then some—on the next trip. Probably no different from a lot of gamblers. Stay in the casinos long enough and eventually they will empty your pockets That's why the drinks are free while you're playing: they want to keep you happy and preferably inebriated.

I was an incredibly easy mark. They didn't even have to ply me with alcohol. I'd just sit there playing blackjack at one of the high-roller tables—just me and the dealer, one-on-one—playing all night long, pausing only to reach into my pocket and flip open the top to my tube of Xanax, and shake loose a couple of tablets. I'd have nothing stronger than Coca-Cola on the table in front of me, so no one had any idea that I was stoned out of my mind. But how else to explain what happened on one particularly memorable night that spring? It certainly wasn't the kind of thing that one would do in a healthy or sober state of consciousness.

Today, a decade later, I could still walk right back to the exact seat at the exact table at the Bellagio hotel and casino, where the craziness began, for the location is burned in my memory. I sat there for hours, sipping Coke and discreetly popping pills, while the stack of chips in front of me continued to grow. At one point I did a quick and rough calculation. I was up approximately $190,000, which was a pretty respectable chunk of change. Certainly I had never come close to winning that much money at the blackjack table. But the winning gave me no great sense of elation or accomplishment, or even an awareness that I'd been spectacularly lucky. I felt peaceful, like there was no pressure at all—no pressure to play basketball, or to be a good father or partner, or take care of my money or my health. I was just sort of numb to all emotion and feeling.

"You're having quite the night, sir," the dealer said to me.

I stared at my chips, a multicolored miniature city of plastic high-rises.

"Yeah . . . I guess so."

I didn't feel the slightest urge to stop playing. I felt nothing at all. It was like I had melted into my seat. So I popped the top on my Xanax bottle, took a couple more pills, and . . .

"Deal the cards," I said. It was like having an out-of-body experience, like I was standing by the table, watching this poor, pathetic, drug-addled soul throw his life away.

Needless to say, I gave it all back. Every penny of it. I kept playing until the chips were all gone, and then I bought some more and kept playing, until I had reached my credit limit with the Bellagio: $100,000. That's right: a $290,000 swing. From up $190,000 to down $100,000.

Before the night was over I hit roughly another half-dozen casinos. I'd made enough trips to Vegas and had enough of a reputation as a high roller that I had secured a strong line of credit at multiple casinos, usually between $100,000 and $200,000. By the end of the evening I had exhausted all my credit. I was down more than $800,000. Tack on the $190,000 I had been up at one point, and you're talking about a one-night loss of nearly a million dollars. I'd had bad nights in Vegas before, but nothing even close to this. In the past, even when I was drunk, I had always walked away before the damage became unmanageable. But the Xanax robbed me of all inhibition, common sense, and reason. It was like I had performed a pharmacological lobotomy on myself while in the middle of an epic night of blackjack.

It was breathtaking.

It was surreal.

It was devastating.

I remember leaving the last casino at the end of the night in a state of stunned disbelief. I'd chewed perhaps forty Xanax since I first started playing that night, so to say that I was sober would be wildly inaccurate. But I was keenly aware that I'd been through some sort of a life-changing experience.

This is not good, Vin. This is not good at all . . .

At thirty-four years of age, I was smart enough to know that I was very close to the end of my career, and certainly past the point where any team would pay me superstar money. I was a well-educated man. I had a college degree. I understood the basics of financial prudence and responsibility: always take in more than you pay out, income should exceed expenses . . . that sort of thing. Economics 101. But, like so many professional athletes, I had failed to exhibit any sort of restraint or logic in my personal life. People often wonder how a professional athlete can go broke—especially one who was fortunate enough to be among the highest-paid players in his league. But it happens. Here's the basic problem: you think the money will never go away. In those years of spectacular earning power, you should be putting away three-quarters of your income, investing it wisely and conservatively, so that it will be there, hopefully compounded nicely, on the day your body calls it quits and forces you into retirement. Instead, you spend like an idiot, burning through every penny you make, as if you'll always have a seven- or eight-figure salary.

Many professional athletes make the mistake of not thinking ahead, of not planning for the future. They believe they will be forever young, blessed with preternatural talent and unlimited resources. Doesn't work that way. Everyone gets old and banged up. It always ends badly. The trick is to realize all of this far in advance, and to plan accordingly—as opposed to throwing it all away on drugs and alcohol, on gambling and women and catastrophic business investments. I lost my spirituality and my connection to the church fairly early in my professional basketball career, but believe it or not, I continued to see myself, and to think of myself, as a God-fearing person. Some people thought this was the height of hypocrisy, but I believed it to my core. Through all the drinking and drugging and gambling and whoring, I felt like God was watching over me, and that eventually he would come to my rescue.

I had no idea that it would take so long—that before he

rescued me, I would be stripped of everything I owned and deemed precious. And I'm not just talking about material possessions; I'm also talking about family, friends, health, spirituality, and dignity.

Everything that makes us whole and human.

In my case, financial ruin stemmed less from hubris than from inattentiveness, fueled primarily by substance abuse. I blame only myself for the fact that I managed to go broke despite earning roughly $100 million. I know it sounds implausible, but it can happen. It does happen. I've been there, so I know. And when I left Vegas that night, I remember a sinking feeling in the pit of my stomach, as I considered the possibility that I might actually have trouble paying back the debt I had accrued at each of those casinos. I had five children to support, along with their mothers. I had multiple homes and cars. I had burned through millions of dollars thanks to alcoholism, drug addiction, gambling, and myriad bad investments.

I was in deep trouble.

WHILE THE VEGAS DEBACLE WAS lurid and sensational, and probably represented the last nail in my financial coffin, it was not the biggest mistake I made. It merely came along at a time when I could least afford such a loss. Less than one year earlier, when I was recently sober and just beginning to get back on my feet, I succumbed to an urge experienced by many celebrities: I decided to open a restaurant.

Have you ever seen the movie *Midnight Run*? There's a scene in which a mob accountant played by Charles Grodin tries to dissuade a hard-edged cop portrayed by Robert De Niro from pursuing his lifelong dream of opening a restaurant.

"I have to tell you, a restaurant is a very tricky investment—over half of them go out of business in the first six months," Grodin says. "If I were your accountant, I'd have to strongly advise you against it."

To which De Niro replies, "You're not my accountant."

Grodin sighs. "I realize I'm not your accountant. I'm just saying . . . if I were your accountant . . ."

I did not have a nagging accountant in my ear preaching frugality. I had investors and business partners and financial advisers who were only too willing to assist in my self-ruin. Thus was born Vinnie's Saybrook Fish House, in my hometown of Old Saybrook, Connecticut. The restaurant actually opened in 2005, in between my stints with the Rockets and Clippers. I was trying to look ahead, to think of that time, which seemed to be coming fast, when I'd no longer be able to make a living playing basketball. That moment finally came in 2006, when I signed a free agent deal with the Minnesota Timberwolves. I was looking forward to playing for Dwane Casey, who had been an assistant coach while I was in Seattle, and who was now the head coach of the Timberwolves. The idea was that I would come in and play short minutes and maybe offer some guidance to the younger guys. But I never got the chance. My basketball career was beyond the point of salvaging. I was thirty-five years old, with a lot of miles on the engine. The Timberwolves released me on November 13, 2006, without my having appeared in a single game. I never played another minute in the NBA.

The thing about being a professional athlete is that you get old fast. But when the gig ends, suddenly you're young again. Thirty-five is ancient in the NBA, but it's not even middle aged in the real world. I had to find something else to do with my life, something to fill the days and feed my ego. In a way,

I felt like the pressure had been lifted from my shoulders. I didn't have to worry about living up to expectations anymore. I could focus on other things. But I still needed money to support my lifestyle—I needed a reason to get up in the morning. So, with the encouragement of my accountant, I began pouring money into Vinnie's Saybrook Fish House. I built the place from scratch. It was a big, beautiful restaurant, two stories high, with a massive fish tank as a centerpiece. A high-end fish house catering to a well-heeled clientele.

What could go wrong?

I'll say this: Just because you enjoy dining out or cooking at home does not mean you should own a restaurant. It is a brutal and unforgiving business. I pumped more than $4 million of my own money into Vinnie's before we even opened the doors, and it floundered from the get-go. I mean, we did okay for a couple of months because of the novelty effect, but that wore off quickly and soon it became just a place to dump money. Tens of thousands of dollars every month going in, and virtually nothing coming out. Since I was no longer collecting a paycheck from the NBA, panic set in. I began drinking again, and got arrested for drunk driving in June 2007. (I pleaded guilty to a lesser charge of reckless driving, but that's a subtle distinction; I was inebriated, primarily because of the amount of Xanax I had ingested.) I soon fell into all the old habits: drinking and gambling (in the form of casino visits and foolish investments) and self-pity. No more than a couple of days after I got my DUI, I totaled my Mercedes-Benz by crashing into a guardrail. I was taken to the hospital after that one and somehow managed to avoid not only a serious injury but also a criminal charge.

This time there was no safety net. My parents supported me, emotionally and spiritually, and even financially, as much

as they could, but everyone else slipped away. Being broke
makes you less popular. I lost contact with Shawnee and our
children in 2007. In 2008 the bank foreclosed on both my
restaurant and my home. I'd made more than $100 million
in my career, and now I was flat busted. People hear that and
find it impossible to believe: *How could anyone go through that
kind of money? He must have something left over.* Here's how
it works. When you're burning through money the way I
was, you don't even realize the enormity of it. I know better now: I watch every penny I earn, keep a careful budget,
and live within my means. But back then? I had no clue, no
restraint, no common sense. By the time I realized the scope
of my financial wreckage, it was too late. See, in order to lose
$100 million, you have to go screaming right past zero and
into the negative column. You don't lose $100 million; you
lose $110 million . . . or more. It's catastrophic waste.

Life unraveled with cold and callous indifference after
that, with one bad day leading inexorably to the next. I cared
only about dulling the pain with alcohol. I tried getting high
once, smoking weed for the first time in years, and wound
up right back in the emergency room, my heart clawing its
way out of my chest, EMT workers signaling ahead that the
patient was in trouble.

"Imminent doom," I heard one of them say at one point.
And then again: "Imminent doom."

Terrifying as that episode was, it didn't provoke any sort
of epiphany, aside from the realization that I couldn't smoke
weed. So I kicked the weed and the Xanax, did a few more
halfhearted stints in rehab, and went back to heavy drinking, primarily Bacardi 151. Those stints in rehab were nothing more than a way to temporarily end the physical pain. I
wasn't committed to the process. I had no real desire to do

the hard spiritual and emotional work required of a sober life. In fact, I wasn't even committed to staying sober in rehab!

At one treatment center I was given Librium to help with detox. Librium is similar to Valium or Xanax and permits an alcoholic to be weaned from alcohol while minimizing painful and potentially fatal withdrawal symptoms. But Librium is also a mood-altering substance, of course, and therefore subject to potential abuse. This should not be an issue in a hospital or treatment center, but given the devious nature of many addicts, it does in fact happen.

I liked the feeling of Librium, not just because it eased my withdrawal symptoms, but because it got me a little high. Eventually I found another patient who was in for treatment of another type of addiction, but who nonetheless was receiving twice-daily doses of Librium. I befriended the guy and he agreed to give me some of his medication. This was not a simple matter, as all medication was distributed by a nurse. We were required to put the medication in our mouths and swallow it in full view of the nurse, and to then open our mouths afterward to demonstrate that it had been ingested. If you were lucky and clever, you could beat the system by holding the pill under your tongue and pretending to swallow.

"Look, bro," my new friend said after successfully completing this task. He spit the tablet of Librium into his hand and held it out. We were sitting in a group therapy meeting, supposedly focusing on our sobriety, and instead we were making a drug deal. "Go ahead. All yours."

He put the pill in my palm. I was disgusted. The pill was wet and beginning to dissolve. As desperate as I was for another hit of Librium, I couldn't bring myself to swallow it. I thanked him for the effort and slipped the Librium into my pocket. After group, I flushed it down the toilet.

Good thing, too. I later found out that my friend, an intravenous drug user, had been diagnosed with hepatitis C. Had I swallowed that tab of Librium, I almost certainly would have contracted hep C, which is one of the most contagious diseases. Considering that I was an alcoholic, and that I went right back to drinking when I got out of rehab, the consequences would have been catastrophic.

I lived mostly with my parents or drinking buddies in those days. I had no relationship with my old college girlfriend and the mother of two of my children, aside from conversations between our lawyers related to the child support payments I could no longer afford to make. Shawnee was more sympathetic about my financial situation, although she, too, had quite reasonably decided that I was no longer fit to be a part of her life or the lives of our children.

Most of the time I felt utterly alone, and then out of the blue, someone would extend a hand and offer to help. Rashard Lewis, a teammate in Seattle, found out I was hurting and immediately wrote me a check for fifty thousand dollars. No questions asked, no expectation that I'd ever repay him. While the money helped pay for living expenses, much of it went to drinking and gambling. I figured out somewhere along the line that I was trying to kill myself. I wasn't the type to buy a gun and blow my brains out, or to intentionally run my car off the road, but I was perfectly content to drink myself to death.

It hurt too much to be alive. I couldn't connect with people. I couldn't generate any purpose in my life.

I couldn't see a way out of the blackness.

15

★　★　★

THE PRODIGAL SON

The amazing thing is that I never spent a night in jail. Through all the episodes of drunk driving, the procuring of prescription narcotics through illicit means, the missed child support payments, the passing of bad checks (yes, I did that, too, a couple of times, quite deliberately, but no one ever pressed charges)—I somehow managed to avoid any serious interaction with law enforcement. Perhaps it was divine intervention. I'm careful about invoking the possibility of that sort of thing, for I believe that God has enough on his plate without worrying about whether I have a soft landing every time I stumble.

Yet there is no disputing my good fortune not just in surviving the mess that I made of my own life (and of the lives of so many around me), but also in the resurrection that I have been so blessed to receive. I believe God bestows on us free will and holds us accountable for our actions, but I also think he is willing to open his arms to anyone who seeks help and forgiveness, and who is willing to undertake the work to set things right.

It's something of a cliché in the world of addiction treatment to say that asking for help is the hardest and most important step. It's also not really true. I asked for help (or at least accepted intervention) multiple times without really meaning it, simply because it was a way to at least temporarily end the misery and to get people off my back—to accommodate doctors and attorneys and employers. In other words, to stay one step ahead of trouble. True change, though, comes only with diligence. It is emotionally and physically exhausting. It is spiritually transformative.

It's also worth it.

From 2008 through early 2011, I was utterly adrift, existing but not really living. Whatever money came in—for example, a $100,000 settlement from the new owners of my restaurant, who changed the name and politely asked me to stay out of their way—quickly went right back out. For all practical purposes, I was completely broke. I moved into the modest home in which I had been raised, while my parents stayed in the more spacious home that I had purchased for them many years earlier. I rarely left the house, preferring instead to simply sit alone in my living room, watching television (until the cable was turned off) and drinking myself stupid. Weeks and months passed in a blur. At some point I stopped drinking Bacardi 151 and went back to Hennessy, rationalizing the move as a step toward healthier living. Not sobriety, though. Not even close. I just knew that 151 would kill me sooner. Hennessy I could drink all day.

For the last six months of my life as a drinker, I put away between a gallon and a gallon and a half of Hennessy every single day. Aside from what it did to my body, I couldn't afford the habit. Hennessy at the time cost nearly fifty dollars for a one-liter bottle, and I needed at least four or five a day just to stave off the effects of withdrawal. So, you're looking at a two-hundred-dollar-a-day habit, or roughly fifteen hundred dollars per week. It's fair to say that every penny I had went toward drinking. And when I ran out of money, I'd sell stuff, which is how I ended up pawning the old tires out of my mother's Mercedes.

There is no act too humiliating for the addict, no deed that will shame him into sudden remorse and a different way of life. He thinks only of the next fix, and of how he can avoid the pain that accompanies an absence of his drug of choice. I judge no one, because I have been this low. I know in my heart that the gap between me and the wretched soul who sells her body for a twenty-dollar hit of crack or meth is almost too small to be measured. Different drugs, different methods of obtaining a fix. Same outcome.

A slow and steady slog toward death.

Eventually it got to the point where I couldn't take the pain any longer. For six months, beginning in mid-October 2010, I started every day in the same exact manner—with a swig of Hennessy, a mouthful of food, and several minutes of ferocious nausea and vomiting. I'd need a good half hour to an hour just to recover from the physical ordeal, and then I could start drinking again. I hardly ate at all, which is why my weight slipped to 190, some sixty pounds below my NBA fighting weight. I'd shuffle around the house all day, in slippers and sweats, one hand clutching a glass filled with Hennessy, the other holding on to the waistband of my pants, to keep them from falling down. From the neck down I was skeletal, but my face was bloated and puffy, except for my eyes, which had sunk into my skull and had taken on the ghastly yellow pallor of a man who is flirting with cirrhosis. I couldn't sleep on my back, because the pressure caused intense pain in my liver. I developed sores in my mouth and throat, a by-product of the corrosive effect of chronic vomiting. Sometimes I'd vomit blood instead of bile, which freaked me out at first but eventually just became another symptom of my descent into alcoholism.

There was psychic pain as well, the steady drumbeat of loneliness and depression. I hated my life. I hated myself. I couldn't stand the misery any longer, and despite my best efforts to drink myself to death, my body refused to give out. Instead, it just doled out pain on an epic scale, day after fucking day. Unable to endure it any longer, I finally surrendered. I gave up. I asked God for help, and then I called my father, and together we drove to the Rushford Center, a rehabilitation hospital in Middletown, Connecticut. I drank on the way to rehab, not because I lacked commitment, but because I physically needed to drink. I'd been through the drill before, several times, and knew that a bit of time could pass between my arrival and the first dose of medication designed to stem the tide of withdrawal, so I wanted to make sure I was well oiled before I checked in. My father glanced at me as he drove and did not even respond to my drinking. My dad is a hard man, but he's also a spiritual man, a preacher, and he could see the depth of my pain. If this is what it took to get me on the road to recovery, it was a small price to pay.

"I'm never drinking again after today," I told him.

"I know, son. I believe you."

This was not an empty promise. I had made a commitment to God and to myself to lead a different life, one based in spirituality and honesty and service. My father was the only person left who would listen to me, the only one willing to distinguish bullshit from a sincere desire to change. There was no one else.

Only my dad.

Part of this was paternal love, but it also stemmed from the fact that my father was a deeply religious man. He knew from being a pastor that there was a higher power, and that by turning my life over to that power, I could find redemption. Dad believed in me; he believed in the power of the holy spirit, and the possibility of change.

"You can do this," he said on the drive to Rushford.

I didn't need to hear that, but I *liked* hearing it.

Even then, with a bottle of cognac between my knees, I was excited about the prospect of starting over. But I had to fix my broken body first; I had to go through detox, clean out my system. Once that was accomplished, I knew I'd be okay. I knew it was true. I felt it in my heart. I was done with drinking. I was ready to put it all behind me. I had died in every way but the physical, and if I didn't clean up my act, that was coming, too. I entered Rushford battered and beaten, but with a sense of spiritual determination I had never known. I walked through the doors accompanied only by God, armed only with prayer. I had no expectations of what life would be like afterward; I just knew that I wanted to be alive. Every other time I had gone through rehab, it was because I was trying to work an angle of one sort or another. This time my motives were pure. I wasn't doing it to save my job or to meet the terms of a contract. I wasn't doing it for the Celtics or for John Lucas, or even for my family.

I did it for me.

Until I took care of myself, I couldn't possibly hope to take care of anyone else. I wanted to be a dad, to get back into the lives of my children, but that wasn't possible unless I was sober and healthy.

This was my fifth attempt at rehab and ultimately one of the shortest. It also was the one that worked. It worked because I had experienced a fundamental change in attitude. On every previous attempt at rehab, I merely went through the motions. I was ashamed, lonely, resistant to treatment. My ego got in the way. I wasn't truly ready to embrace sobriety. This time, emboldened by a desire to serve God, I had made up my mind. I was all business when I walked through the doors of Rushford. No swagger, no aliases, no con jobs. I was there to get clean and sober. On the very first day, when they came into my room at three o'clock in the morning to distribute medication and take my vitals, I was already awake.

"Let's go," I said. "I'm ready."

On any of my other trips to rehab I would have greeted the staff at that hour with a grumble and a sour face. I would have pulled the blankets up over my head and pleaded, "Leave me alone."

Not this time. I was eager to get to work. The sooner I got healthy, the sooner I could leave and get on with my life and my ministry. It was that simple. It was that clear.

Unlike in my previous stints in rehab, I did a lot of listening this time. I'd always been the talker, trying to fake my way through treatment with charm. After a while I'd get comfortable and be honest about my story. I'd tell everyone that I was a professional basketball player, and that I was an alcoholic, but there was as much bragging as there was contrition.

This time I tried to keep my mouth shut, not because I didn't want to share my story, but because I thought I could learn more by listening to others. People knew who I was, but I didn't make a big deal about it. It didn't matter anymore. I had been humbled. I wanted to be quiet. I wanted to take care of the business at hand, as opposed to turning rehab into my own personal show. The irony of it is, I knew the drill; I knew the right things to say. I knew what was expected and what would have played well. None of that mattered anymore. This time it was in my spirit.

The first few days of rehab were all about survival. I was a very sick man, trying to recover from years of self-abuse. My existence had depended entirely on alcohol, and now I was paying the price yet again. Like everyone else going through detox, I wandered the halls like a zombie, withered by my own pain and suffering. But I'd been through this before and I knew that it would end soon enough. I avoided the conversations and camaraderie that help make the experience bearable for many patients—the sharing of war stories and the dark humor that marks conversation outside a formal group setting. A lot of the patients were smokers. On break they would all go outside together and share cigarettes. I was not a smoker, which gave me an easy excuse to pass up these interactions. In the past I would have jumped in. Now it was merely a distraction that I did not need.

There's something that happens after a few days in rehab, when the body begins to clear itself of toxins. We call it the "pink cloud." It happens to almost everyone—a euphoric feeling of freedom and clearheadedness.

Oh, my goodness. I'm sober! I'm going to stay this way forever!

I'd been in the pink cloud several times, and it always produced a false sense of security. This time I would not be fooled. When the pink cloud lifted me up at Rushford, I did not overreact. It was just part of the process.

They gave me Librium again, but I viewed it strictly as a tool to facilitate my goal—a release from the pain of addiction. Three days into what was supposed to be a thirty-day program, I began telling the staff that I would be out in roughly a week, as soon as I had completed detox and was out of danger. They'd heard this sort of thing before, usually from patients who were either scared or lacked commitment, or both.

"Vin, you've been down this road," one of the therapists said to me. "If you leave early, you'll go right back to your old life. We both know that."

I didn't argue with her. She had every right to feel that way. She had the wisdom that comes with experience, and she knew my personal story. But I had something else: faith.

As much time as I spent in group and individual therapy at Rushford, I spent even more time in prayer, and reading my Bible. I asked God to give me strength. I asked for one more chance. I vowed not to let him down again.

In rehab, doctors and therapists generally have nothing against religion or spirituality; they just don't believe in miracles, or even shortcuts. They believe in science. They believe that healing takes time and diligence, particularly if the patient has already relapsed multiple times. I understood their concern. But this time was different.

I was different.

I wasn't at Rushford because I was trying to save my basketball career or because I had violated the terms of a contract. There was no employer or union standing behind me, ordering me to complete a certain level of treatment or face dire financial consequences. I had nothing left. No money, no career, no home, no family. I was far beyond the point where anyone wanted to stage an intervention on my behalf. I wasn't worth the effort. I was beholden to no one, and that made it all a little bit easier. I had entered Rushford because I wanted to be there. This was the first time I ever went through rehab without a single visitor or phone call, in part because I wanted it that way, but also because there weren't many people who knew I was there, or who would have cared anyway. It was just me saying, *This is it. I'm going to get sober.* There were no conditions to it. I found that liberating and empowering.

I was alone, and because I was alone, there was less push-back from the staff than there would have been in the past. The Celtics weren't checking up on me. The NBA had long since stopped caring. Rushford didn't even have to contend with meddling family members. Without any sort of outside pressure, there was only so much the staff could do to coerce me into a longer period of treatment.

I stayed at Rushford for only a week, just long enough to safely detox. I knew I didn't need thirty days of therapy. I just wanted to make sure my vitals were clear and that I wouldn't have a seizure after I left the hospital. I didn't want to be shaky and craving alcohol or Librium or Xanax. Once I had reached that point, I checked myself out. Technically, I left Rushford AMA—against medical advice. I signed the appropriate paperwork absolving the center and its staff from any liability in the event that I relapsed or suffered some type of catastrophic medical event after I went home.

On the day I walked out, none of the doctors or therapists expressed anger or disappointment. It wasn't like I was the first person who had checked out AMA. Moreover, I had not been belligerent or arrogant.

"I'm ready to go home," I said. "I'm going to be okay."

The same therapist who earlier in the week had tried very hard to convince me that I was making a huge mistake now offered only a smile and sincere encouragement.

"We don't want to see you back here, Vin. We're rooting for you." She paused. "Remember—thirty meetings in the first thirty days."

I nodded. "I know."

I HAD NO IDEA WHAT I would do next; I knew only that alcohol would not be a part of it. I'd been a hard-core drunk for ten years, but that person was dead now. In his place was someone who wanted to get on with life.

My father picked me up the day I checked out. We hugged at the door, although this time the embrace was fueled not just by love but by happiness and hope. On the ride home I started talking to my father about spirituality and how much I missed the church, which had been the foundation for my life—for everything good that happened to me—when I was growing up. I quoted scripture to him, and he soaked it all in without an ounce of judgment. I told him that I had changed, and that I was never going back.

He nodded.

"I mean it, Dad."

"I know you do, son."

"Dad?"

"Yes?"

"I want to go to church with you this Sunday, if that's okay."

He smiled, almost imperceptibly. "Of course."

Until I got sober I didn't realize the enormity of the damage I'd done. I had burned so many bridges in the preceding decade that it was nearly impossible to find anyone willing to accept the notion that I had changed. My drunk charm was gone, along with my money. I reached out to various people to both apologize and reconnect; more often than not, the response went something like this: "Vin, I don't think you understand the magnitude of what you did."

"Yes, I do. And I'm truly sorry. But I'm sober now."

Long pause. "Doesn't matter, brother. Too late."

I may have tried a little too hard to convince people that this time I was serious, that finally I could be counted on. I had to remind myself that I'd been gone a long time. It wasn't like the world was sitting around eagerly awaiting my return, as Shawnee pointed out to me during one of our first conversations after I got out of Rushford.

"Vin, no one cares whether you're sober. You're trying to make this a badge of honor, and it's just not. You've done so much harm. The last thing anyone cares about is your sobriety."

There was so much rubble, so many people suffering because of the choices I had made. I was trying to stop the train, and all around me people were saying, "Too late, the crash already happened." The anger was understandable. It would have been nice for everyone if I had experienced this epiphany several years earlier, like when the Celtics told me to stop drinking. I would have had $20 million in the bank. Now I was crawling from the wreckage while everyone around me was dying.

I had no right to expect anyone to celebrate.

Ultimately, I went back to the one place where they had

to take me: Full Gospel Tabernacle in Old Saybrook, the church in which I had grown up, and where my father was still a minister. I had a lot of work to do in order to fix my life, but I figured it had to be built on a foundation of sobriety and spirituality. If I could remain healthy and connected to God, I'd be okay. I could handle anything else.

I went to church the following Sunday, just a few days after getting out of Rushford. I wanted to keep a low profile for a while, but my father was so excited to have me back that he decided to introduce me to the congregation. Full Gospel Tabernacle is a small church, but the place was packed that day. My father looked out over the congregation and basically told them that the prodigal son had come home.

"I took my son to rehab. He was there for a week, and now he's back! Stand up, Vin."

I slowly rose from my seat, raised a hand of acknowledgment, and felt the eyes of the crowd on me. I looked at the faces, some of which I recognized. There was a mix of appreciation and confusion.

Wait a minute. How long was he in rehab? A week?! And now he's okay?

It probably seemed implausible to just about everyone except my father and me, and only one of us understood that it was a bit too early for a grand entrance. But Dad believed in me. Buoyed by the power of the Holy Spirit, and the unwavering love of a parent, he welcomed me back into the fold in a very public way. The problem was this: Dad had invoked my name on numerous occasions over the years, often from the pulpit. He would describe my struggles and then proudly announce that I was in treatment and getting help. And then I would relapse. I don't doubt that some people began to tune him out after a while when he talked about my supposed rebirth. It's only natural for people to be skeptical, just as it is only natural for a father to never lose hope.

"Dad, I don't mean to be ungrateful," I said after church that first day. "But you have to understand—I've been to rehab five times. It might be best not to talk about that part of it too much. I went there because I wanted to physically get better. I didn't go there to be cured of addiction. Spiritually, I made a commitment, and I'm going to trust in God. I'm going to pray. And that's how I'm going to get better."

Dad nodded. "I understand."

I don't mean to sound preachy, but the fact is, I am a preacher—a licensed minister. It's just that my evangelism now is less about standing in the pulpit than it is speaking with youth groups and others who have faced struggles similar to my own. I'm not a fire-and-brimstone kind of guy, but I do believe that by sharing my story, and demonstrating that recovery is possible, I've found meaning in life. Fame is fleeting, fortune is a lie. Without friends and family and a connection to something bigger than ourselves—community, society, God—we are lost. Buoyed by that connection, we can endure all manner of tribulations, and accomplish almost anything.

For me, the first steps back to a whole and normal life involved recovering my health and spirituality. I knew how much damage I had done to my body and mind. Drinking had destroyed my foundation. I knew that I had no shot at rekindling a relationship with God unless I healed my mind and body. That's why it was so important for me to get into rehab: not as a long-term fix, but as acute care. Getting sober was just a part of the bigger picture, which was getting closer to God and restoring my relationship with him.

It took strength and prayers to go into rehab. But my

goal, and my plan, was different than it is for many people who enter rehab. I'm not saying it's the best course of action; I'm just saying it worked for me. In AA they talk about the importance of sticking with the program after you get out of rehab—getting to thirty meetings in thirty days, for example, finding the right sponsor and leaning on him or her for advice and support. I think that's great, and I understand why it has been such an effective program and helped so many people over the years. But I was getting so much from church that I just felt like that's where I needed to throw all my energy and purpose. I don't have anything against AA meetings—I went to a few when I got out, and found them supportive and beneficial. For me, though, it wasn't the right vehicle. I needed something more intense, something from a spiritual and theological standpoint.

Nothing about my fall or recovery has been anonymous. I'm certainly not going to suggest that fame makes it harder to maintain sobriety, but it does complicate matters. Look, I'm not asking for pity. I accept full responsibility for my actions, and I know that I'm not the first public figure to become an alcoholic or a drug addict and lose all his money. It happens, and a certain degree of schadenfreude can be expected. If you're stupid enough to lose $100 million, you shouldn't expect much sympathy, especially if alcohol, drugs, and gambling contributed heavily to the loss. But I was committed to recovery and I wanted to go about the process differently, in a way that made sense for me personally. I had to put the process of physical and emotional restoration before the process of redemption. As soon as I felt healthy and physically free of the craving of alcohol, I jumped headlong into reconnecting with my church and, by extension, with God.

Full Gospel Tabernacle conducted Bible-study classes every Wednesday night. I became a fixture. There were Sunday school and traditional church services on the weekend. And there were other opportunities as well. I tried to get to at least four church services a week in an effort to restore my relationship with Christ and with God. It's strange—I had never been at a lower point in my life, and yet I was filled with hope and optimism. I had lost everything—money, fame, livelihood, family, dignity—but in God's house I was not judged; I was accepted. In church, at least, I had a fighting chance, and it quickly became my refuge.

For the better part of a month I sat quietly in a pew and listened to the services. I read the Bible with a fervor I had never known. I was raised in the church, but like a lot of kids had not felt a personal connection to the messages I heard. They washed over me and gave me a blueprint for behaving appropriately and honorably in a world that does not always value these things, but the connection was tenuous. Now it was different. Scripture and parables spoke to me in a way I'd never known. They reached into my heart and into my soul, as if to say, "This is about you, Vin. Are you listening?" And I was. Intently.

One day after Sunday services I approached my father with a proposition.

"I'm ready to teach, Dad."

He was skeptical at first, not because he doubted my sincerity, but simply because I was still in the early stages of recovery. The wounds were still raw, and in that state it's not unusual to get carried away with the possibility of a new life, and yet be unable to follow through when the novelty wears off or when things get hard again. Moreover, I had no background in teaching or preaching, aside from the fact that it was the family business. But my worthiness stemmed less from theological wisdom than it did from practical, real-world experience, and from personal testimony. I figured that by merely standing up in front of the congregation and telling my story, I would have something to offer.

"Are you sure?" Dad said. But he said it with a smile, so I knew he actually liked the idea.

"Yes," I said. "I feel like I've come back from the dead, and I want to share that feeling. I know that the process of restoration and redemption, starting with me praying and having faith in God, could heal me from addiction. I want to share that message."

Testimony of this sort—in which a layperson takes over the pulpit—is not embraced in all churches. But Full Gospel Tabernacle, while located in the Northeast, is clearly rooted in the spiritual tradition of fellowship common in Southern Baptist churches. I was allowed to stand up in front of the congregation and talk about my journey. This wasn't easy, of course. I'd grown up in this church. I knew these people. They were my friends and family. I had been a hero to them, a local boy who made good—who took all of God's gifts and put them to use in a positive way. And then I lost everything. I had squandered God's generosity, which is often viewed as a sin of the highest order. I had no idea how people would respond to hearing my story.

As it turned out, they welcomed me back with open arms. I really was the prodigal son! I had come after years of wandering, after years of self-destruction and moral decay. Instead of being rejected, I had been embraced by my father.

And by my Father.

All I wanted to do now was repay my debt, and the only way I knew how to do that was by sharing my story, by baring my soul in the hope that it might offer encouragement to others who were lost or struggling.

I had returned to the church in part because the church was my family, and I needed their support and acceptance and love. I went back to Full Gospel Tabernacle to strengthen myself. All the rubble that I had created—with my career and with fans and teammates and organizations—mattered not in the least once I walked through the front door of that church. I couldn't go back to the life I once had, and I didn't want to go back, anyway. The church was a place where I could rediscover *who* I was, as opposed to *what* I was. It was a place where I could be quiet, and I could listen, and the spirit of God could move me, and manifest itself in my life without any distractions, without anyone saying, "Oh, he lost it all. What's wrong with him?" I wasn't worried about anything other than my spirituality and my health. The financial wreckage? It didn't matter. That was going to unspool in an ugly way for at least the next five years, and there was nothing I could do about it. And frankly, I did not care. A lot of people who once were wealthy and then become poor never recover. They stew in self-pity or beat themselves up over mistakes they have made. Mainly, they just miss the comfort they once knew and the lifestyle they once had. Ego becomes an enormous obstacle to acceptance and recovery. From the moment I returned to the church, I didn't feel that way. Whatever pit I had thrown myself into, I knew there was only one way out: not by scheming or dreaming about reclaiming lost wealth and fame, but rather through cultivating humility and spirituality.

I was there to heal, and I did that by telling my story over and over, and by starting every testimony with an expression of gratitude for where I was in the healing process.

"I'm sober today. It's been thirty days since I've had a drink. And I thank God for that."

To me, the freedom was miraculous. The fact that I did not even want to have a drink was bigger than Peter walking on water. Not too long ago I had a conversation with my father about the fact that my six-year anniversary was approaching. I haven't thought much about time lines and milestones since I stopped drinking, but this one hit me hard.

"Dad, do you realize I will be six years sober on April 17? And I've never thought about going back."

It's that last part that stops me cold, that fills me with wonder. In five years of sobriety, not only have I not relapsed, I've never even felt close to a relapse. I say that not with arrogance, but with a deep sense of gratitude. I feel like I've done the work necessary to remain sober, but I also know that many people still feel the pull of addiction, still think about what it would be like to have just one more drink. And I wonder why I've been so fortunate to escape that temptation. The only thing I can think of is that for me, the approach that works is one that involves committing to a higher power.

I can't do any of this on my own. I won't make it without God in my corner.

16

★ ★ ★

ABYSSINIAN BAPTIST CHURCH

Let's talk about miracles.

No, not the big kind—like the parting of the Red Sea or the healing of a terminal illness. Miracles come in many shapes and sizes, and defining something as miraculous is often just a matter of perspective.

Take, for example, something as simple as food. In my last couple of years as a drunk, I barely even gave it a thought. Perpetually sick and exhausted, inebriated or hungover, I often went days without a legitimate meal. In the last few months of my alcoholism, I barely ate at all, becoming malnourished and cirrhotic along the way. Food got in the way of drinking. It smelled bad, it tasted bad, and it took up space in a belly that wanted only alcohol.

As the craving for liquor subsided and the toxins were slowly removed from my body, I began to notice something. I could smell food from a great distance, and it smelled fantastic! Didn't matter what it was: anything from a salad to a platter of ribs, it all looked delicious. Only an alcoholic or a drug addict can truly understand what I'm talking about—the way all needs and desires are superseded by the single-minded pursuit of getting high. For the longest time, nothing mattered to me except the next drink. My body demanded only alcohol. Now, suddenly, I'd get up in the morning and eat a massive breakfast: eggs, bacon, pancakes. Whatever. Three hours later I'd be eating again. Dinner was a feast. Naturally, I began to put on weight. At first it was good weight—weight that needed to be restored to my skeletal frame. Within a couple of months I looked like a relatively normal, healthy man. And a few months after that, I looked like maybe I was enjoying the process of becoming reacquainted with food a bit too much. I didn't care in the least. On the few occasions when I would look in the mirror and notice I didn't exactly look like a professional ballplayer, I'd hear God whispering in my ear.

Relax, son. You're not playing basketball anymore. Don't be self-conscious. That's a trick of the enemy.

Without basketball, there were no expectations. All I had to worry about was getting better and staying sober. For nearly a year I didn't really do anything as far as fitness or conditioning were concerned. I didn't play basketball or go to the gym to work out. It was all about spirituality and strength. For me, it was enough to wake up in the morning clearheaded and unburdened of the desire for liquor. If a side effect of that was a spare tire around the middle, well, there were worse things in life.

My only worry was that I had five children and virtually no contact with any of them. I waited several months before even attempting to reach out to Shawnee, with whom I still maintained at least a cordial relationship. We weren't close, for she had been put through a terrible time because of my drinking and various other indiscretions. Shawnee was happy for my sobriety, but it took a while before she was willing to allow me back into the lives of our children. There was so much hurt and so much pain, because when my financial demise came, it affected not only me, but also everyone around me, especially my kids. Shawnee had to work hard to hold things together. She accepted food stamps; she borrowed money so that she could pay the water bill and the electric bill. She did what she had to do in order to take care of her kids. She was angry with me and hurt. I cringe even now at the thought of what I put her through. I will forever remain grateful that she allowed me back into her life, and into the lives of our children.

It was the fall of 2011 when Shawnee and I began speaking regularly. The conversations usually centered on our kids, with me asking for updates and anecdotes, trying not to seem desperate or demanding. I wanted to rekindle my relationship with them, but I knew I had no leverage whatsoever, no right to ask for anything. All I could do was cling to my sobriety and continue to lead a healthy and spiritual life, with the hope that eventually Shawnee would see that I really had changed, and that my intentions were pure. It was a lot to ask. Financially, I had virtually no resources, so it wasn't like I could improve their lives through monetary means. I had nothing to offer but my love and support. The thing that gave me hope was Shawnee's innate goodness; she is a compassionate woman whose family has struggled with addiction issues. Ultimately, she came to believe that I was committed to sobriety, and that building a relationship with our children would not only help me in that regard, but would also be beneficial to them as well.

I began spending time at Shawnee's house, getting to know our three children. And for the first time in my life I understood the meaning of unconditional love. I had little to offer aside from my time, but that seemed to be enough. Pretty soon we were seeing each other several days a week, and I'm proud and grateful to say that my kids have been the most important part of my life ever since.

I wish things had worked out as well with my other two children, but that relationship has been more challenging. Their mother took me to court shortly after I became sober and accused me of hiding money and failing to provide adequate financial support. There was no money; I was beyond broke. Nevertheless, a settlement was reached and I have done my best over the years to meet the terms of that settlement, but the anger and bitterness continue. And that saddens me. It hurts terribly that I don't have much of a relationship with those two children, because I've spent some time with them—mostly when I was drinking—and they are beautiful kids. I'd like to repair my relationship with their mother so that I have an opportunity to give them what my other kids have seen: A sober father. A spiritual man who has something to offer.

Money remained a problem in those early days, though I tried not to become overly stressed about it. I figured that if I could stay clean and sober, eventually opportunities would come my way. A conversation with Charles Smith, a retired NBA player, led to an invitation to take part in an overseas tour in December 2011 sponsored by the newly formed Professional Basketball Alumni Association. It seemed like relatively easy money: travel to China and play a series of low-key exhibition games in front of adoring fans who would not be offended that we were all long past our prime. A promotional poster for the event listed the stars in descending order of fame and popularity. At the top, in the largest letters, were the future Hall of Famers Dennis Rodman and Scottie Pippen. On the next line, in a slightly smaller typeface, were Penny Hardaway, Gary Payton, and Clyde Drexler. Then came Larry Johnson, Cliff Robinson, Mitch Richmond, and Dale Ellis. My name was on the bottom line, in type so small as to be almost unreadable.

I was not really bothered by it. For me, this was a purely mercenary venture—a chance to make some money, pay off some debts, and help support my children. My contract included a stipulation that I would not drink. There was some partying on that trip, but I was not involved. I saw evidence of it only in the aftermath, on buses that carried us around in the morning hours. One day, for example, some of the boys were joking about what a hard night it had been, and how they were feeling a little worn out. I smiled and tried to make light of the situation.

"Glad I wasn't there."

A couple of the guys smirked and laughed, as if to say, *Yeah, we know how that turned out.*

I was the NBA player who blew it all. Even among my peers, I was considered a train wreck. In a previous life, in those situations, I was the life of the party. Now I was the punch line of a joke.

I could handle that. What I couldn't handle was the actual physical exertion associated with returning to competitive (or even noncompetitive) basketball. On a roster populated by guys who weren't exactly in peak physical condition, I was the softest. I thought I did all right, all things considered. But after we returned from the trip I got a call from Charles Smith.

"Listen, Vin," he said. "I'm going to be able to get you on more of these trips, but you've got to be in better shape." He paused, and then he hit me hard. "Seriously, man. You've got to shed some of that fat."

Under different circumstances, an assessment that blunt might have broken me and sent me right back to the bottle. This time, though, it barely scratched the surface. Immediately, I started eating differently, watching my calories, and getting to the gym on a regular basis. There was no pressure; I did it because I wanted to be healthy and to feel better about myself. If the by-product was a chance to take part in another tour, great. If not, well, at least I'd be fit, and that was a good thing

IN EARLY 2012 I MADE a call to Howard Schultz. Howard had been an owner in Seattle but was no longer involved in basketball by this time. We had always had a good relationship, but basically we were boss and employee. I'm not even sure why I called Howard or what I expected. He was a smart and generous man, and I figured maybe he'd have some thoughts on what opportunities might be available.

He returned my call on a Tuesday night. I was in my car at the time. When I saw the number light up, I pulled over quickly and parked on the side of the highway. My heart was in my throat as I said hello.

"Vinnie!" Howard yelled, like we were old college buddies or something. "How are you, my friend?"

And just like that, the anxiety melted away.

"I'm doing well, Howard. How are you?"

"Very good, and Starbucks is doing fine."

I didn't know what this meant. I had forgotten the path that Howard had taken, that he had left Starbucks and the company had struggled a bit, only to recover when Howard returned.

"That's good to hear, Howard."

"Thank you, Vinnie. I must say, you sound great."

I laughed. "Well, I'm just trying to piece things back together, sir. It's a big job."

"That's okay, Vinnie. I understand. What can I do for you?"

I wasn't looking for a handout. I sought information . . . guidance . . . mentorship. In return I would offer Howard a better version of myself than the one he used to know. We talked for a while and then agreed to meet the following month in New York, along with Howard's wife, Sheri, and their son, Jordan. At the time I was working part-time for the Bridgeport Housing Authority, doing outreach with inner-city youth. And I was coaching a middle school basketball team. I was grateful for the work and for the opportunity to fill the day with productivity. But it wasn't enough to pay off the debt I had incurred or to support my children.

"Tell me what's really going on, Vinnie," Howard said when we got together in New York.

I gave him the abridged version, much of which he already knew. I stayed away from the gory details, and tried to focus instead on how well I was doing spiritually. I talked about my church, and the peace I had found.

"Howard, everything spiraled out of control," I explained. "I started making bad business decisions with my restaurant. And I kept drinking. With New York, I kept drinking. Even in the settlement with the Celtics, I kept drinking. But I knew that God would pull me through this. I could feel his power and his strength. And I'm happy at church now. I know God has a plan for me. I just need a way to make a living."

It went on like that for a while, with me referencing God and faith in every other sentence. Finally, after about the tenth time I used the word "God," Howard interrupted me.

"Vinnie, do you believe in God for everything?"

I hesitated. Was this a trick question? I wanted to answer honestly without detracting from the fact that I needed help financially.

"I don't know about *everything*, Howard, but I do believe I'm getting an opportunity to get back on my feet because of God. I believe I'd be dead without him. Absolutely."

Howard nodded. "Okay . . ."

A couple of hours later, when I got back to Old Saybrook, Howard called. He sounded upbeat.

"I think we have something for you, Vinnie. We've put a lot of thought into this and it feels like the right fit."

I was so excited! My mind began racing, thinking about the possibilities. Maybe Howard was going to set me up with some kind of partnership, put me in charge of a dozen Starbucks shops, with an option to buy in through sweat equity. I'd be a retail magnate in no time! Or maybe he'd put me on the corporate fast track. Howard was a powerful man; anything was possible.

Anything . . .

"There's a church in Harlem—Abyssinian Baptist Church. Are you familiar with it?"

Abyssinian was nationally renowned, so I had at least a passing familiarity with the church. But not much more than that.

"Dr. Calvin Butts is the pastor there," Howard continued. "He's also a friend of mine."

"Okay," I said. I had no idea where any of this was going.

Howard gave me the name of one of Dr. Butts's assistants. "I want you to reach out to her. Tell them we talked. They will be expecting your call."

I was very confused, but didn't want to sound ungrateful. "That's great, Howard. I can't thank you enough. But . . . what exactly am I calling about?"

Howard laughed. "You need a job, right?"

"Yes, sir."

"Well, start by telling them that."

As soon as I got off the phone, I began doing research on Abyssinian Baptist Church and the esteemed Dr. Calvin Butts, who was not only Abyssinian's pastor, but also the president of the State University of New York (SUNY) College at Old Westbury and an influential leader in the African American community. I did some reading about the Abyssinian Development Corporation, a rather powerful entity in Harlem, and realized that Dr. Butts was a powerful businessman as well as a religious and academic leader. The assistant with whom I spoke, as it turned out, was technically an employee of Abyssinian Development, which led me to believe that I was being considered for some type of job within the corporation, probably something to do with public relations or community outreach. It seemed like a good fit and made perfect sense.

It was also an erroneous assumption on my part.

We met in Dr. Butts's office in Harlem a couple of weeks after my phone call with Howard. I had done my homework, so I knew much more about Dr. Butts by this time—enough to be appropriately impressed and even a bit intimidated. He tried to put me at ease, but like Howard, he controlled the conversation in a way that left me feeling somewhat disoriented.

"So, Vincent. Tell me about yourself," he said. "What brings you here?"

"To Abyssinian?"

He smiled and shrugged, and I got it. He wasn't asking how I got to Harlem, or to Abyssinian. He wanted to know how I had reached this point in my life. I wanted to ask, "How much time do you have?" but instead I gave him the abridged version. We talked for a while; the conversation twisted and turned, touching cryptically on matters of faith and spirituality, of community and education. The one thing we did not talk about was business or employment. Most of the research I'd done was on the Abyssinian Development Corporation, so I was prepared to pitch myself as a strong candidate to join that organization. I thought it would be good and interesting work. I also thought it would provide a decent income and help me get back on my feet and provide for my family.

Dr. Butts had something else in my mind, although he was slow to release the information. I left that meeting with no job offer and no idea whether I'd ever return to Abyssinian.

"Let's stay in touch," Dr. Butts said.

We talked again a few days later. There were more trips to New York to discuss my possible role within Abyssinian, and slowly I got the idea that he wanted me to be part of the church, not Abyssinian Development. He eventually made a call to my father and revealed his plans—before he had even told me.

"I want Vin to be my youth minister," Dr. Butts said.

My father swelled with pride, forgetting for a moment

that I had never really preached. My experience at Full Gospel Tabernacle was restricted to Bible study and offering testimony as a layperson. I was a man of faith; I had returned to the church. But I was no preacher. That didn't stop my father from offering a glowing recommendation.

"He's ready to go," Dad said. "He's been running all along."

All of this occurred without my knowledge. "Dr. Butts gave me a call the other day," my father said, as if it was no big deal. "We talked about you becoming the youth minister at Abyssinian."

"Really?" I said.

"Yes. I told him you'd do a great job." He paused, smiling proudly. "And you will."

I was scared to death at this prospect, but I also needed both a job and something worthwhile to do with my life. Abyssinian would meet both of those needs. It was an incredible opportunity, and one that I figured, in my naïveté, would likely offer significant compensation. Youth minister at one of the most famous churches in the United States. It sounded like a prestigious position, one that carried with it a great deal of responsibility. But it wasn't really a job. It was more like an academic fellowship, the parameters of which I was slow to grasp.

For more than a month after my initial meeting with Dr. Butts, I drove into Harlem twice a week, for services on Wednesday evening and Sunday morning. Dr. Butts wanted me to get a feel for the church, to understand what services looked like, and to meet some members of the congregation. I had no formal role whatsoever. I was merely an attendee. Each trip was an emotional and financial drain. I was nearly broke, barely able to scrape up enough money to pay for gas and tolls for the ride from Old Saybrook to Harlem. The first time I sat in a pew at Abyssinian, my heart sank as the collection plate came my way. I watched as people, many of whom were of limited means, filled the plate with tens and twenties. Or fifties. I fumbled for my wallet. Inside was maybe thirty or forty bucks. I swallowed hard, removed all but a few singles, and placed it on the plate.

That I had reached a level of such impoverishment was unknown to Dr. Butts, as it was to almost everyone else. Howard had told him of my struggles, but I don't believe he understood the extent of my collapse. One day after service he took me around Harlem to visit some older members of the church. This was something Dr. Butts did from time to time. He would reach out personally to parishioners who, for reasons of age or infirmity, were unable to attend service. His energy was boundless and his commitment to Abyssinian and its members unflagging. We were standing outside a brownstone, waiting for someone to answer the door, when Dr. Butts gave me a hard look.

"So, Vin. Can I ask you something?"

"Sure, Dr. Butts."

"You lost . . . everything?" His expression was a mix of disbelief and compassion.

I shrugged. "Yes, sir."

"Really? I mean . . . *everything?*"

I'd been through this before. How do you explain losing $100 million? Dr. Butts could see that I was neither lazy nor unintelligent. Addiction notwithstanding, how on earth could anyone burn through that kind of money?

I shifted my weight nervously from one foot to the other. A flush of embarrassment came over me.

"Well, not everything," I said. "I've still got my car. Got the house, too."

Dr. Butts smiled. He seemed relieved. He did not know that the house belonged to my parents, or that the car, a somewhat ridiculous, gas-hogging burgundy Lincoln Navigator, had been paid for in cash some time ago, when there was still cash to spare. Right now, at this moment? Standing on these steps? I had nothing. But I was too embarrassed to admit it.

The following Sunday I was finally introduced to the congregation at Abyssinian. It was daunting. The church was filled to capacity, as it usually is on Sundays. Abyssinian is a beautiful and historic landmark, so in addition to having thousands of members, it is also a popular tourist destination. The congregation at Sunday service is an eclectic mix of locals and visitors from all over the world. In front of this audience Dr. Butts stood up and welcomed me to the fold.

"I want to introduce our new youth minister. He's a friend of Howard Schultz." Dr. Butts paused and put out a welcoming hand. He smiled at the crowd and then at me. "Please say hello to former NBA superstar Vincent Baker."

Loud applause filled the church as I made my way to the front of the room, to stand alongside Dr. Butts. I could feel the sweat forming on my collar. You think shooting free throws in the playoffs is pressure? Try walking out of Rushford and into Abyssinian with only a few months in between. Standing at the front of a monumental church, in historic Harlem, less than a block from Adam Clayton Powell Jr. Boulevard. With the eyes of a sprawling, throbbing congregation on you.

Now that's pressure!

That I was able to do this without passing out in front of everyone was partially a credit to my experience as an

Olympian and a professional athlete, and a survivor of the disease of addiction. Mainly, though, it was a credit to Christ and my faith. I didn't make this journey alone.

I even felt a little swagger in my step, which really wasn't a good thing. I was only a few months out of rehab, still in the early stages of recovery. Humility was paramount; I didn't want to be treated like a celebrity, and it wasn't healthy. At the same time, I understood that Dr. Butts was trying to make me feel good, while also making it clear to the church that I was not just someone he had pulled off the street. Most of the youth ministers at Abyssinian came to the position with a wealth of experience, having already been pastors at megachurches. It was a high-profile job that required both experience and attitude.

I had neither, so Dr. Butts did his best to infuse me with a little of both.

"Take a good look," he said to the crowd. "I get 'em handsome!"

Laughter, more applause. It felt almost like I was back in the NBA, getting introduced with the starting lineup. Except I had done almost nothing to deserve the accolades. Ready or not, I was in the spotlight.

"Welcome to Abyssinian, Vincent," Dr. Butts said. "Why don't you say a few words to the people."

I kept it short and simple.

"Thank you. I'm Vin Baker, and like Dr. Butts said, I'm the new youth minister here at Abyssinian. I'm very grateful for the opportunity."

That was about it. I was on and off in less than a minute. This was neither the time nor the place for a sermon, or to tell my long and complicated story. There would be plenty of opportunity for that.

I SPENT NEARLY THREE YEARS at Abyssinian, attending seminary and working as a youth minister. I did not earn a penny, but neither did I incur any debt, as the Starbucks Corporation picked up the tab for my education and living expenses. This was Howard Schultz's version of tough love:

> *If God is the most important thing in your life, then let's maximize that relationship. Let's see how hard you are willing to work.*

It was a test of faith and friendship. I didn't know Dr. Butts on a personal level, but I did know Howard, and I trusted him; I knew that whatever he put his hands on seemed to blossom. His success and compassion were obvious. Whatever he wanted me to do, I was going to do it, no questions asked.

Howard's relationship with Dr. Butts, I learned, had been formed several years earlier when the Abyssinian Development Corporation became involved in the relocation of a Harlem Starbucks. Anything related to business or real estate in New York can be contentious and complicated, but this particular project wound up facilitating a friendship between Dr. Butts and Mr. Schultz. On the surface, I suppose, they may have appeared to have little in common: the Jewish businessman and the black pastor of one of the most historic churches in the country. But as I got to know them both, I began to see how much they had in common, not just in terms of their devotion to the concept of community but in terms of the way they saw things. Both Howard and Dr. Butts are capable of thinking way outside the box. It can be disconcerting and confusing at first, but once you spend some time with them, it can be downright inspiring.

Howard made it clear that he had gone to great lengths to arrange for my time at Abyssinian, and that he expected a full commitment in return.

"I'm taking this very seriously, Vinnie," he said. "I expect you to do the same."

The implication was that Dr. Butts was taking a chance on me based on the personal recommendation of a friend and business associate. Reputations were at stake. I had let Howard down in the past; I couldn't do it again.

By the time I settled in at Abyssinian, my mind-set had changed from one in which I was focused on trying to figure out how I would earn a living to simply furthering the strength of my spirituality. I was essentially a student, working at Abyssinian and taking classes at Union Theological Seminary (which was affiliated with Abyssinian). It provided me a place to live and food to eat. I threw myself into classwork and into working with youth groups at the church. It was an amazing and invaluable experience, one in which I learned as much about myself as I did the people with whom I worked.

Addiction was the eight-hundred-pound gorilla in the room. For a while at Abyssinian, I was Vin Baker, the former NBA all-star who had apparently decided to choose a dramatically different career path. I wasn't sure how much people knew about my downfall, or when and how it would be appropriate to share the details.

The first time I mentioned alcohol in front of a congregation, I did so in a lighthearted manner, casually referencing "that strange-tasting eggnog we all have at Christmastime," as part of a larger sermon addressing questionable behavior and habits. It was meant to be a joke, a way to introduce a delicate subject with which I had enormous personal experience. I wasn't the kind of minister who worked off a manuscript back then (I'm still not, although I have learned to take a bit more time in preparation), and my words were not chosen carefully. The joke fell flat, both with the audience and with my boss. When the service ended, Dr. Butts called me into his office. This was something he rarely did, so I had an inkling that he wasn't happy.

"Vincent, I want you to stay away from the drinking references," he began. "I know what you were trying to do, but that isn't the way to go about it."

I explained that, given my history, it might be time to start weaving into my work a few examples of my own life.

Dr. Butts nodded. "Everybody knows," he said. "And you are not the only person in this church who struggles with that issue—"

"Right, that's my point," I interrupted. "Maybe this can help."

Dr. Butts rubbed his forehead in frustration. "I agree. But not like that. If you want to deal with it on a very personal level, which can be difficult, then go right ahead. You have to be willing to do it in a helpful, honest way. Otherwise, don't go there. It's not funny."

Dr. Butts was absolutely right. I had been tone deaf. I wanted to connect with the audience in a way that I felt would be meaningful. I wanted them to understand that I wasn't an NBA superstar. Not anymore. I'd been through something terrible and, through the grace of God, I had come out on the other side. I understood that most people, including the members of Abyssinian Baptist Church, could not identify with the notion of losing $100 million. But surely they could identify with the concept of loss, and of the powerlessness that comes with addiction. I tried to broach this subject because I knew it was on their minds. I could see it on their faces every time I walked into church.

What happened to him?

Is he okay?

No, I wasn't "okay." Like everyone else, I was struggling. I was broke and trying to find my way. But I was alive. I was sober.

That's what I wanted to share. I just didn't do it very well that day.

The more time I spent with Dr. Butts, the more I came to admire and respect him. Our relationship was not only that of mentor and student, but also somewhat that of parent and child. It was a lot like my relationship with Howard. Dr. Butts believed in me and supported me, but he also challenged me.

One day during the first couple of months, I made the drive from Connecticut to Abyssinian for a midweek meeting with some church representatives about the possibility of running a series of basketball clinics and camps. The meeting was in a different section of Harlem that I did not know well. As is often the case in New York, parking was a nightmare. I was trying to save money, so I drove around for quite some time looking for an on-street parking space, rather than paying for a garage. Eventually I found a spot several blocks away, and rushed over to the meeting, barely arriving in time. In my haste, I forgot to make a note of where I had parked—a big problem, considering I didn't know the neighborhood well.

Afterward, I wandered around for nearly an hour, growing ever more flustered as the vehicle avoided my eyes. You would think a burgundy Navigator would stand out like a . . . well, like a burgundy Navigator. But it didn't. I started to wonder whether it had been stolen, and even considered phoning the police for help. Finally, after about an hour, I found it. Then I moved the car closer to Abyssinian so that I could attend an evening funeral service.

After the service Dr. Butts called me into his office.

"What were you doing down on 127th Street this afternoon?"

I stiffened at not only the question, but the way it had been delivered—in a somewhat accusatory tone.

"I had a meeting about some camps," I said. "And then I lost my car."

Dr. Butts leaned back in his chair. There was a long pause. "What do you mean you lost your car?"

"Just that. I couldn't remember where I parked."

Another long moment of silence.

"Vincent, how are you doing with that other stuff?" he asked.

That's when it hit me: Someone had seen me many blocks from church, wandering around like I didn't know what I was doing, and had reported the observation back to Dr. Butts. And he had become concerned that I'd relapsed.

"I'm fine, Dr. Butts. Really. Totally sober. You don't have to worry about that."

"Well, that's good to hear."

I had to swallow a bit of righteous indignation. It was understandable that Dr. Butts would be worried; my track record, after all, was not great.

"Someone told you they saw me, huh?"

He shook his head. "No, I drove by and saw you myself. Wondered what you were doing."

There was an awkward moment in which neither of us knew what to say. Then, almost simultaneously, we both burst into laughter.

"You know, Dr. Butts," I said. "You could have offered to help. Might have saved me forty-five minutes."

THE BEST PART ABOUT MY time at Abyssinian was working with children; it was a much less complicated matter. The children in the youth program were generally preadolescent, from roughly ages seven through twelve. These kids didn't go home and Google the life story of Vin Baker. I didn't avoid the subject with them, but neither did I make it the center of conversation or focus on the lurid details. In general, their response to me was purely visceral and unfiltered.

"Oh, my God, Mr. Baker. You are so tall!"

I enjoyed being around the kids, and I loved preaching to them, partly because it was an opportunity to revisit some of my favorite stories from the Bible. It wasn't enough merely to reference, for example, David and Goliath. I had to digest the story myself, be clear in its meaning and interpretation, and then find a way to present it in a simplified manner to a very young and impressionable audience with an extremely short attention span. It was fun and challenging, and I loved every minute of it.

Abyssinian was simultaneously the most rewarding and challenging period of my professional life (and my spiritual life). However, it was not a sustainable lifestyle given my personal situation. I still had five kids and bills piling up back home. There were moments of crisis, when I'd be lying on the bed in my sparsely appointed Harlem apartment, feeling the weight of the world on my shoulders. But even in those hard times I did not feel alone. I knew I had two of the biggest bodyguards standing behind me: a billionaire coffee mogul and one of the most powerful figures in the African

American community. They believed in me. I had to believe in myself. I had to have faith that the hardship was merely part of God's plan. Sometimes, when wracked by doubt, I'd play in my head a song by the Reverend James Cleveland, "I Don't Feel No Ways Tired."

I don't feel no ways tired,
I've come too far from where I started from.
Nobody told me that the road would be easy,
I don't believe He brought me this far to leave me.

On a couple of occasions, just as I was ready to bail, money seemed to fall from the sky. First, my parents sold the home in which I had grown up. My mother took the $90,000 gained from that sale and put it into her bank account and parsed it out to me in dribs and drabs over the course of a year. She did not have to do that; the house was in my parents' names and it was theirs to do with as they saw fit. I hadn't yet earned the degree of trust that would allow her to give me the full amount all at once, but they wanted to support me and my new life.

A second windfall came in the form of a settlement between the NBA Players Association and the NBA involving shared proceeds from licensing revenue. Turns out there were a handful of players who were owed money—and I was one of them.

"How much?" I asked when the call came in.

"Sixty-nine thousand dollars," was the answer.

I almost dropped the phone. There was a time, at the height of my playing career, when I made more than that in a week. Now, though, it was a princely sum, more money than I had seen in years. The timing was fortuitous, not just because I desperately needed the cash, but also because now I was smart enough to spend it properly. The settlement could have occurred two or three years earlier, when I was in the depths of alcoholism. I would have immediately squandered it on booze and gambling. Now I had the strength and sense that came with sobriety.

When I asked how soon I would receive the check, I was told I could pick it up right away, at the union office, which was located on 125th Street in Harlem, just a dozen blocks from Abyssinian. As I walked down the street, practically floating on air, I couldn't help but feel as though God had somehow put this right in front of me when I needed it most. I was in a space so spiritual and trusting that there was no way you could have convinced me it was merely a coincidence.

I nearly broke down in tears at the sight of the check. The uncomfortable juxtaposition of financial need and spiritual growth was corrected. The desperation had been at least temporarily lifted. I could support my kids, pay my bills, and focus on my ministry.

I LEFT ABYSSINIAN AND Union Seminary in the spring of 2014, roughly twelve credits shy of a master's degree. The circumstances surrounding my departure were somewhat controversial, and not entirely in keeping with the teachings of the church.

In the course of rebuilding my life and reconnecting with my children, I naturally began spending some time with their mother. I never stopped loving Shawnee. Our relationship had been fractured by my selfish and impulsive tendency toward self-destruction. There had been periods of extreme anger and frustration on her part, but only at the very end of my alcoholic spiral did she completely shut me out of her life and the lives of our children. I don't blame her for that; it was an act of self-preservation. But as I slowly cleaned up and began spending some time with the kids, and demonstrating a commitment to be the best father I could be, things changed. Given the financial constraints of my current condition, my means were limited, but whatever I had, it went to my family. This was important, for it proved to Shawnee that I wasn't just doing the Christian talk. Actions speak louder than words, and I was doing everything I could to make things right.

Shawnee began to soften. The truth is, I admired her enormously for taking care of our kids in my absence. I am ashamed that I didn't do more to make their lives easier, but there is no undoing the damage; all I can do now is demonstrate clarity and purpose. I am no longer a wealthy man, but I am a sober man who wants to be a good father.

And a good husband.

Neither of us expected this to happen. It was as natural and organic as anything could be. We were spending lots of time together—I would visit whenever I got some time off from my work in Harlem—almost always in the company of our children, and as sometimes happens between two people who have so much shared history, a romantic relationship blossomed.

Again.

One day Shawnee called me.

"Vin," she said. "I'm pregnant."

I was speechless. I was also filled with a sense of happiness and possibility. I felt blessed.

But this was complicated.

I had committed my life to Christ, and to spreading his

message. I was a high-profile youth minister at a high-profile church, and I had gotten my girlfriend pregnant out of wedlock. This was what is sometimes referred to as an untenable situation. I could not continue to teach and work at Abyssinian. I knew what the rules were, and how we were supposed to live, and I knew that I had violated the rules. I had failed to live in a manner consistent with the teachings of the church, and I was a prominent face of the church.

I left Abyssinian and came home to Old Saybrook. Shawnee and I had a very calm and grown-up conversation. I immediately suggested marriage as the only sensible course of action. Shawnee and I had become friends, and were on the way to falling in love all over again. We would have four children now, and I wanted to be there for them every minute of the day. It all seemed so logical. Shawnee, however, was somewhat hesitant.

"It's been seven years since we've been together," she said. "A lot has happened. What if it doesn't work? We aren't kids anymore."

"I know that," I said. "But we're here now, in this situation, and this makes all the sense in the world. And I love you."

I wanted to be with her despite all the craziness in our lives. I was in love not just with Shawnee, but with our whole family and what it represented. I grew up in a family with both parents, and my parents are a big part of my life to this day. They're everything to me. I wanted my boys to have that as well.

Eventually, over the course of several weeks and many long conversations, we came to an agreement. We would get married. For the first time, we would be a legitimate family. This did not please everyone in my circle, especially some people at Abyssinian. But to me the moral transgression (if you want to call it that) was in fact a blessing. I don't play God. I know the rules, and I know what's spoken about in the Bible, but Shawnee's pregnancy was one of the best things that ever happened to me.

17

★ ★ ★

STARBUCKS AND SECOND CHANCES

left Abyssinian as an ordained, licensed minister, and with
a greater understanding not only of my spirituality, but also
what it means to be an evangelist. My wife had a good job
as a school counselor. To help make ends meet, I was able
to negotiate a settlement with my former financial adviser
that provided bridge funds for a period of time. Still, money
remained tight—so tight that I even joined Dennis Rodman
on his infamous trip to North Korea. That was sad and surreal (I saw in Dennis the same issues with alcohol that once
plagued me, and in the North Korean leader Kim Jong-un I
saw, and met, a dictator whose repugnant record of human
rights violations speaks for itself), and I regret having done
it. But I needed the paycheck, so I held my nose and got on

the plane, justifying my role as a global spokesperson for the sport of basketball. No harm, no foul, I figured.

Eventually, in the spring of 2015, Howard Schultz came to the rescue with yet another dose of tough love. At the time, I was basically a full-time stay-at-home dad, driving the kids around, making meals, cleaning the house, and coaching the basketball team at Cutler Middle School, where my son Kameron was a student-athlete. I loved being around the kids (especially my son) and teaching basketball to youngsters who played purely for the love of the game. Unfortunately, coaching middle school basketball did not pay the bills. One day I got an e-mail from Dan Pitasky, a human resources executive at Starbucks.

Dan's message came completely out of the blue. Several months had passed since I had parted ways with Abyssinian. Since I left a few credits shy of a degree, I didn't know whether Howard was disappointed in me. I certainly didn't expect him or anyone from Starbucks to reach out. The e-mail was somewhat cryptic, though casual and friendly. Dan wanted to know how I was doing and whether I would be interested in discussing some possible opportunities within the organization.

"Have you ever thought about retail?" Dan asked.

I didn't hesitate. I also did not lie. "Honestly, no," I said. "What do you have in mind?"

"We're wondering if you might consider working for the retail division of Starbucks. Management trainee."

I was so excited about the opportunity that I didn't even think about the reality of the offer—what it was going to be like to walk into a store and pour coffee for strangers all day long. I was just happy that Howard hadn't dumped me and left me for dead. In essence, this call represented Howard saying, "Let's give him another shot."

"Dan, I will do anything," I said. "Just tell me what you want."

Shortly after Memorial Day, I met with Peter, a regional manager, and Beth, a store manager, at a Starbucks in North Kingstown, Rhode Island. Since this was where I would be working, we had the meeting in the store. It was not what I expected. We went over my schedule, talked about what the job would be like, and then we embarked on a lavish tasting session. This was the essence of the Starbucks experience, they explained—developing an appreciation of the product by identifying and understanding the nuances of Starbucks coffee. There was just one little problem:

I was not a coffee drinker.

That's right. Through all the years of alcoholism and drug addiction, I had somehow managed to avoid developing a caffeine habit. It wasn't that I disliked coffee; it had simply never become a part of my daily routine. I didn't know good coffee from bad coffee, Sumatra from Sanka. It was all the same to me: a strange and bitter brew whose appeal completely escaped me. I was way out of my element when we sat around a table and began sampling various strains of coffee. This was an exercise in which all new Starbucks employees were expected to participate. Since most of the staff are experienced coffee drinkers, they enjoy the process. For me it was weird and awkward. Small cups of coffee were distributed. I watched as Beth and Peter swirled their cups gently, and then sniffed the aroma with their eyes closed, in exactly the manner of a wine tasting. I did the same, despite feeling rather silly.

"Put a small amount under your tongue," Peter said. I did as instructed. "Now hold it there for a second. Let it breathe. Good, right? You get that faint taste of citrus?"

I swallowed hard, coughed a little, and then nodded. "I think so."

Peter and Beth laughed.

"I'm sorry," I said. "I'm not much of a coffee drinker."

"That's okay. You'll learn."

I sure did. It's not possible to work at Starbucks and re-main neutral or ignorant on the subject of coffee; nor is it possible to work there without embracing the company cul-ture. One of the questions I was asked during the hiring pro-cess was this: "Why do you want to work at Starbucks?"

Although I was an addict for many years, and had ac-quired many of the unflattering traits that come with that designation—such as an ability to lie and deceive others, as well as myself—I am an inherently honest and candid person. The first thought that went through my head when presented with this query was, *Are you serious? I want to work at Starbucks because Howard Schultz is my friend and former boss and he's trying to help me out. I need a job.*

That would not have been the right response. My inter-viewers wanted to know what drew me to the company from a philosophical standpoint. In many cases, the people who are hired by Starbucks are longtime customers who not only need a job but also have a legitimate fondness for the brand based on years of being loyal customers. They know how to answer this question. I did not. But I gave it my best shot.

"Starbucks is a great company, and I'd like to be part of it."

There is a culture of commitment and customer service at Starbucks that from the outside may seem a bit too precious, but it's nonetheless genuine. Believe me, you have no idea how much thought and effort go into that venti dark roast you order every morning—from the beans that are harvested in Africa all the way to the preparation at your local store.

It's serious business. I found it rather intimidating at first, but once I bought into it, a career in coffee was born.

As with Abyssinian, it was a heavy dose of immersion therapy. There was no tiptoeing into the water. One day I was home in Connecticut, coaching basketball, the next day I was taking meetings in the Starbucks offices, and then I was behind the counter, wearing an apron and waiting on customers, with virtually no idea what I was doing. I learned quickly, simply because there was no other choice.

I became a management trainee at the North Kingstown Starbucks. Beth went easy on me the first day, and gave me an 8:30 a.m.–to–4:30 p.m. shift. Mornings are treacherous at Starbucks. Most stores open as the sun comes up to prepare for the prework rush, and traffic is relentless for several hours. By 8:30, things have settled down. Business escalates again in the evening. I missed the heaviest congestion that first day, which was a blessing not just for me but for the customers as well.

To say I was clueless would be an understatement. I did not know a macchiato from a mocha. I didn't know how to run the register. All I could do was help out behind the counter by filling cups with ice or by cleaning up and organizing supplies. I spent a lot of time just watching and trying to learn. When the shift ended, I was exhausted, both mentally and physically.

And that was on a slow day.

After a week or so things got much more intense. I had to learn how to take orders and run the register. There was a very specific protocol for everything. I had to learn how to work the drive-through window, which is probably the most daunting job at Starbucks. Roughly 75 percent of the drink orders at Starbucks are customized—"skinny," "half-caffeine," "no whipped cream," and so forth. At the drive-through window, these orders come fast and furious. It's almost like speaking a foreign language. I had to get every word exactly right, or face the unblinking stare of an irate customer. And I had to do it with a smile and a script.

"Welcome to Starbucks, can I take your order?" I said when I first got behind the drive-through microphone.

One of my coworkers, who was tutoring me that day, waved his hands in admonishment.

"Bro, that's not even close."

"Yeah, I'm sorry."

"Repeat after me: 'Good morning. Thank you for choosing Starbucks. What can I get for you today?'"

I wrote it down on a piece of paper, just to make sure I wouldn't forget. But after a few customers, it became automatic. Getting orders right was a bit more problematic. One of my first customers at the drive-through peppered me with a complicated order. Several different drinks, all different sizes and customizations. I stood there at the console, staring at what seemed like a thousand buttons, each denoting a different variation, and tried to hit the right ones. Sweat began to bead on my forehead as the customer kept firing away. It was like she was trying to mess me up. I felt like I was on the free throw line at the end of a close game, with the opposing fans waving crazily behind the basket.

"You got all that?" she asked impatiently, her disembodied voice high and anxious.

"Yes, ma'am."

I did not have it all. Not even close. As she rattled off her order I had tapped away at the buttons in a blind fury, hoping for the best. When she pulled around to the drive-through window, I felt a surge of nervousness, for I knew the order was wrong and that the customer would be understandably upset. As the car approached, I looked into the driver's window. There, behind the wheel, smiling broadly, was Beth, my manager.

"Gotcha!" she shouted.

I let out a sigh of relief and laughed. "I'm sorry, Beth."

"That's okay. It gets easier. Trust me."

One of the things that I loved about my experience at Starbucks, especially in North Kingstown, was that I had to depend on so many people. It was truly a community workplace. Being a comanager with virtually no experience, I had to depend on every employee simply to get through the day. It was a reversal of the usual arrangement. Subordinates did not kiss up to me, I kissed up to them. But my affection for them, and my need for their assistance, was real. My humility was real.

Despite the fact that I was a manger—a boss—I had no idea what I was doing. I hadn't come up through the ranks; instead, I had been placed in a position of power and superiority based on my friendship with Howard. I had to be very careful about how that would play out on a daily basis, within the cramped and pressure-packed confines of a busy retail operation. I was smart enough to realize I needed help. And I didn't mind asking for it. I deferred to the greater experience and knowledge of my coworkers, and they responded in kind. As a result, we developed incredibly strong relationships within the store.

"Look, I know I'm supposed to be your boss," I would say. "But I realize you know more about this place than I do. Let's just help each other out and work together."

It was so simple and so true.

I did my job from a place of humility. I didn't walk or talk

like an NBA all-star. If someone—a customer or coworker—
asked me, I was more than happy to chat about hoops. But
this was not a time or place for arrogance. Let's be serious: I
was far removed from sharing a court with Michael Jordan.
There were times when one of my coworkers would ask me
about my playing days, and I'd say, "I'd like to share a story,
but I've got to get these teas done in the next five minutes."
That was the reality of my situation. The past didn't matter.
Only the work that was in front of me mattered.

In every way possible, I was humbled by the job. That's
not the same as being embarrassed. The only time I felt a
twinge of shame was the day Shawnee brought my two sons
into the store, without telling me ahead of time. Vin Jr. was
fifteen years old. He knew of my fall, of course, but only in
the abstract. To him, I was still an NBA all-star; I was his
hero. We shared the same name, the same passion for basketball. And though he had no obvious reaction to seeing me
that day behind the counter, wearing an apron, I felt bad. But
this was my life, and maybe it was good for him to see it up
close. I wanted him to understand that I was working hard
to remake my life, that I was out there grinding, day after
day, trying to support my family and atone for the mistakes
I had made, many of which had affected him and his siblings
profoundly.

Still, there is no denying the truth: it hurt.

SOME CUSTOMERS FEIGNED INDIFFERENCE. Others would cast me a
quizzical or pitying look. Quite a few would smile and shake
my hand and ask me how I was doing. One gentleman even
thought my presence behind the counter was some sort of
elaborate stunt. He stared at me for the longest time be-

fore placing his order. He fidgeted nervously while looking around the store.

"Where's the camera?" he finally said.

"Excuse me?"

"The hidden camera. Where is it?"

"There's no hidden camera, sir. I can assure you of that."

"Come on," he said. "You're Vin Baker, right?"

"Yes, sir."

"Then this must be a prank—one of those celebrity video things. No way Vin Baker is making my coffee."

A full ten minutes passed before I was able to convince him that he wasn't on camera. I was just a guy doing my job.

Eventually my presence at the North Kingstown Starbucks ignited a flurry of publicity. There were newspaper and magazines stories, followed by a predictable deconstructing on social media. The response was overwhelmingly positive, and I was grateful for the support. I was humbled to an extent that most people can't imagine. I saw no shame in working at a coffee shop. And that's the message I wanted to convey. I wanted people to look at me and say, "Wow, this guy got kicked in the ass, but he's not bitter, he's getting on with life. Good for him."

I put everything I had into working as a retail trainee at Starbucks. I had to do it right. I couldn't let down my family. It wasn't about becoming a millionaire again. It was about getting a steady job and a steady income. And there was potential for it to be more, in so many ways. I just had to do it well.

From the very beginning Dan was clear that I had an escape clause.

"Look, Vin, if there comes a time you don't want to do this anymore, let us know and we'll figure it out."

"No, it's fine," I said. "I can handle it."

"Well, there might be some media issues that could be challenging."

"The media?" I said. "I'm old news. They won't care."

The media cared a lot, but in a far more compassionate manner than I had anticipated.

I suppose it would not be a surprise to learn that the first few months on the job nearly killed me. Certainly it wouldn't surprise anyone who has worked in retail. I had no idea what I was doing: how to make the drinks, prep the station, clean up, run the register. Nothing. I was a blank slate. Frankly, it was nerve-racking. But after a while it became second nature. Each day passed by in a blur of activity (a caffeine-fueled blur, I should add; after a while I fell in love with espresso, which helped me get through some of those twelve-hour shifts), at the end of which I would drive home, exhausted but filled with hope and satisfaction.

One of our semiregular customers was a gentleman in his sixties who was a major shareholder in the Starbucks Corporation. He was always dressed impeccably, and whenever he came into the store the staff would get excited and fawn over him like a celebrity. He was quiet and polite, and usually sat at the same table, where he would slowly sip his coffee while reading a newspaper. One day, shortly after a long and thoughtful story about me had appeared in the *Providence Journal*, he waved me over to his table.

"Sit down, Vin," he said.

I pulled up a chair and waited for him to speak. He was the type of man who provoked respect not simply because of his wealth, but because of the way he carried himself. He was dignified and self-assured, but in a quiet way.

"You have a wonderful story," he began. "I think you're

going to do amazing things for this company. But I want you to embrace the job. I want you to embrace what you're doing."

"I understand, sir."

"I'm serious," he added. "I know that Howard has something special planned for you. But I don't want you to get caught up in the story of it, because it won't allow you to live in the moment."

I tried very hard to live in the moment, but I never knew who was going to walk through that door and cause the present to collide with the past. One late-summer afternoon, a man walked in and smiled at me as I prepared to take his order.

"Do you remember me?" he asked.

"I'm sorry, sir. I don't." This was true. I did not recognize the man, or the pleasant-looking woman on his arm.

"Long time ago we got into it. Me and some of your boys. I tried to sue you."

I stared at him, and finally his features came into focus. It was the man with whom I had tussled many years before at my charity softball tournament in Connecticut. He looked somehow younger now, more than a decade later. He looked healthier. I knew this phenomenon because I'd seen it in the mirror. It happens when you stop drinking. Years of self-abuse melt away and the body comes back. Like Benjamin Button, you can almost feel the aging process kick into reverse.

At first, I didn't know what to say. Was he here simply for a cup of coffee? Had he heard about my new career through the local media, and decided to stop in and poke fun at my rather public demise (even though I was grateful for the work and didn't mind sharing that news with everyone)? Was he here to resurrect an old beef? I didn't know, but every possibility left me filled with dread and discomfort.

"Ummm . . . how are you?" I stammered. And then I said nothing, as nothing seemed appropriate.

"I'm good," he said. "You?"

I smiled. "Couldn't be better."

He nodded, put out a hand for me to shake. There was a sense of peace about the man. I got him and his friend a couple of coffees, we said good-bye, and he walked out the door. As I watched him leave, I felt visibly shaken, so much so that I had to go into the back of the store for a few minutes to regain my composure. I'm not exactly sure why I felt this way. Was it relief? Gratitude? Shame? Some combination of the three, perhaps. I honestly don't know.

BY THE FALL OF 2015, I was getting ready to run my own store. Starbucks is an innovative company that provides ample opportunities for employees to advance, but that advancement typically requires expertise acquired through years of on-the-job training. I was managing a store after roughly six months on the job. You don't have to be a genius to connect the dots on that one.

I was lucky to have been given a second chance in life, lucky to have had a mentor like Howard Schultz, who did not give up on me even when so many others had. I tried to do the best that I could with the good fortune that came my way. If I did this job well, I could be a district manager, overseeing five to ten stores. After that, maybe regional manager, overseeing as many as a hundred stores. And from there, perhaps, a move into the corporate offices.

Anything was possible.

Life is hard, of course. But it can also be beautiful and full of hope and promise. At Starbucks I learned all over again how to embrace the hard work and sacrifice that makes it all worthwhile. If I woke up in the morning and went through my old video highlights and newspaper clippings, if I were to dwell on the past and the material things I once had, and the opportunities I squandered, I would likely have lost my mind. Instead, I viewed each day as a gift from God, an opportunity to serve him, and in doing so to take care of the people I love the most: my children and my wife. I took my work seriously. I took my responsibility seriously. I didn't take myself too seriously. Painful as my journey had been, I was able to laugh about it—or at least some of it. I hoped that by sharing my story I could demonstrate to others that there is always hope for redemption.

Never quit.

Never give up.

Life will change—and sometimes for the better.

In the beginning, I would catch twenty, maybe twenty-five people a day making eye contact, giving me a long, hard look, as if to say, *Oh, my gosh, is that him? Is that Vin Baker?* On their faces, I'd see a mix of sadness and surprise. Most Starbucks stores depend on a regular and local clientele, so after a while I became just another guy working behind the counter, but every so often there were interactions that genuinely surprised me. One day a man walked right up to the counter and said, "What are you doing here? You should be on a basketball court somewhere!"

"Thank you very much, but those days are over," I said with a smile. "I'm happy to be here."

For every person who expressed pity or condescension, there were fifty who offered something else . . . something much more meaningful. Like the gentleman who came into the store and, after introducing himself and shaking my hand, proceeded to tell me about his daughter.

"She's going through a hard time," he said. "She has some issues."

"I'm sorry to hear that."

He nodded. "Thank you, but yesterday morning I showed her that story in the *Providence Journal* about you. I handed her the paper and said, 'Read this, hon. It might help.'"

There's a great deal of work and responsibility involved in running even a small restaurant or coffee shop. One morning, for example, I was at the store at four thirty, preparing for a five o'clock opening. Twelve hours later I trudged home, so tired I could barely stand up or keep my eyes open. Days like that were not unusual, but I didn't mind. I was happy that Howard trusted me with the keys to one of his stores. I was proud to lead a small team of employees. It took me only a few weeks as a manager to have a new and greater understanding of what it means to be a coach. Managing a Starbucks is not so different from coaching a basketball team. You have to motivate and teach the people who work for you. It's not a "bossy" job—or at least it's not in the way that I did it. I tried to treat people the way I would like to be treated: with dignity and respect, and with an appreciation for the work that is being done. We were all on the same team, after all. I remember the coaches I admired, and I tried to channel the characteristics I saw in them. It's not my nature to be a screamer, anyway, but I think you accomplish more by urging people to work with you, rather than for you.

After I'd been at Starbucks for a few months, I attended a regional meeting for store managers. There was a lot of talk about teamwork and strategy, and I was struck by how much of it resonated for me, and how it reminded me of being part of an athletic franchise. There was the same blend of hard-headedness and innovation.

"Everyone knows you can't pair a ten-year veteran with someone who's only been on the floor for one month," someone said at one point. "It just doesn't work. Too much frustration."

I was still new to the company at the time, and thus reluctant to speak up in these types of settings. And yet, this comment struck me as being not only representative of narrow-mindedness, but also right in my wheelhouse. I told everyone about my experience with being traded from the Milwaukee Bucks to the Seattle SuperSonics, and what I learned from that experience.

"If there is a culture of winning within an organization," I said, "it can spread to everyone involved, regardless of their experience. You can't be afraid of pairing young people with older people, or putting people together who have very different amounts of experience. It doesn't matter. When I got to Seattle, there was a culture of winning. There were certain things my teammates did that were representative of a winning team. Simply by being around them, and watching them, I became a winner, too. And by adding some new players to the mix, the team stayed fresh and vital and hungry."

I paused, a bit for dramatic effect, but also because I wanted to phrase things carefully.

"That's the way it works in an organization that has a culture of winning, and I think we all can agree that Starbucks is used to winning."

I meant every word of this. I was legitimately happy to be there before the sun came up; I was thrilled to be opening a Starbucks at an hour of the day that I used to consider the shank of the evening. Just to be able to walk into a store in the quiet of the predawn hours, sober and clearheaded, was like a small miracle for me. It certainly represented a life on the upswing.

That's the point: I didn't fall to the level of Starbucks. I was *lifted* to the level of Starbucks!

My life had been turned around, primarily due to the grace of God, but also because of an opportunity from a man named Howard Schultz. I had no problem doing my best to embody the image he wanted for his company. You want a smile with your morning coffee? You got it from me, and it was the most sincere and earnest smile you'd see all day.

COINCIDENTALLY, THE NBA SLOWLY BEGAN reopening its doors to me around the same time I began working at Starbucks. Just a crack at first—but then, an opening is what you make of it, right?

I did a couple of alumni events for the New York Knicks. Then, in the summer of 2015, I took the family to Las Vegas for a week's vacation while I helped out with the Milwaukee Bucks' entry in the NBA summer league. It was an opportunity to work with players, do a little coaching, get introduced to NBA life from a different perspective. That led to an offer a couple of months later to join the team during rookie camp in what amounted to an internship in player development and coaching. When rookie camp ended, there was no job for me, but the team then decided to extend a tryout as a broadcaster. This seemed a strange opportunity, as I had no background whatsoever in that field, but I guess they saw something in me that hinted at potential. I gave that one my best shot as well—again, with absolutely no expectation that it would lead anywhere. And it didn't. The tryout basically amounted to doing color commentary on taped broadcasts of NBA games, and let me tell you something: it's much harder than it looks (or sounds).

So, I was 0–for–2 in trying to land full-time employment with one of my old employers, which didn't really bother me, because I was perfectly content to keep working diligently at Starbucks in the hope of one day getting my own store to manage. As training camp was about to open, I got another call from the Bucks. Jason Kidd, the head coach and a good friend of mine, wanted me to fly to Milwaukee and work with the team in some sort of player development capacity. The duration of my stay was open ended. First, I had to work with Starbucks to secure another week of vacation, which the company graciously accommodated. Then I had to do some serious soul-searching. I was committed to Starbucks and Howard, but if there was a legitimate chance to catch on with an NBA team . . . well, that was like a dream come true, a second chance to spend my life around the game I loved.

I spent a week in Milwaukee, at the end of which Jason invited me to stay for an entire month—basically the duration of the training camp. There would be no financial compensation, and no guarantee of a full-time position when the regular season began. In order to accept this offer I would have had to resign from Starbucks, which on the surface seemed crazy. I was on the management fast track, and I owed something to my friend and mentor. To walk away from that based on the possibility—a possibility not even discussed in concrete terms—of a full-time position with the Bucks just felt irresponsible. It felt wrong.

I think the Bucks saw the benefit in having a former franchise star back in the fold, especially one whose horrific story apparently had a happy ending. I think they felt I had something to offer the young men on their team, not just from a technical standpoint (working with big men), but from the standpoint of a cautionary tale. I had once been a young man with more money than I could handle and an addiction problem that eventually siphoned off every penny and nearly cost me my life. There is no shortage of young millionaires in the NBA, kids who just a year or two earlier were in high school, and for whom drinking and smoking weed feels as normal as can be. Maybe they would listen to someone like me.

I appreciated the Bucks' giving me an opportunity. At the same time, however, I thought a monthlong tryout, without pay, was a bit excessive. I mean, I know where they were coming from. I think they wanted to see me every day, at work, clear eyed and energetic and committed to the job. In other words, they wanted to see me sober, and to gauge whether there had been any long-term damage. I wasn't offended. My record of self-destruction speaks for itself, and I was in no position to negotiate the terms of my NBA comeback. If someone wanted to give me a chance, I would either do what was asked, without complaint, or I would say, thank you very much, but I have to decline.

I explained to Jason and the front office that as flattering as it was to be considered for any sort of long-term opportunity, I couldn't at this point afford to take that big a risk. Practically speaking, I couldn't afford to go four weeks without a paycheck. I wasn't going to do that to my wife and kids. I had worked too hard to establish credibility and trust with them, and I loved them too much to jump off a ledge without a safety net. It seemed selfish and unfair.

Jason was great about the whole thing. He even hosted a little dinner for all the coaches on the day I was leaving, and wished me well and said he hoped we might work together again someday. We were in Madison, Wisconsin, at the time, and in the hotel lobby were posters of the players and coaching staff. My face was on one of the posters! I suppose you could argue that the Bucks really were thinking of me as a long-term prospect. It certainly felt that way to me when I walked through the lobby every morning.

Man. They're really making me a part of this.

But I had no contract. I had no guarantee.

So I went home. The day after I left Madison I was back behind the counter at Starbucks, working twelve-hour days, sunup to sundown. I didn't regret the decision one bit. That first night home I kissed my wife and kids, had dinner with my family, and collapsed into bed.

I fell asleep quickly and deeply, the way you do when you're at peace.

EPILOGUE

Everything happens for a reason.

I truly believe that, and I think about it now, standing in the corner of a high school gym, watching my son Vin Jr. drain a deep three-pointer, his form better than the old man's ever was. He's only seventeen years old but already six foot six, with the skinny, loose-limbed frame of a kid who still has some growing to do, so it's not surprising that he's attracting the eye of college coaches. I'm proud of him, of course, of the way he plays with such poise and composure—but mainly I'm proud of the fact that he is doing everything the right way. He's an honors student who steers clear of trouble, and of the behavior that inevitably leads to poor decisions and regret. I don't harp on this stuff. I don't have to, because I am a living, breathing example of everything that can go right . . . and how quickly it can all go wrong.

Before every game, Vin Jr. joins me in the stands for a few

minutes to go over strategy. We talk about the opponent's strengths and weaknesses, and about focusing on certain aspects of his game that help him stand out. It's pretty simple stuff, and it always ends with me giving him a hug and saying these words: "You may or may not be the best player in the gym tonight, son, but you're the best player to me. I love you. Have fun."

I love basketball, and I love watching my kids play basketball, but it's not about the game, and it's not about whether they win or lose, or how many points they score. For me, the blessing simply is to be a part of it; it's walking into the gym sober and clearheaded. That's what matters. I don't have any other expectations. I know Vin Jr. has big plans, and sometimes I worry that he puts too much pressure on himself. I know it can't be easy to carry my name—there is the burden of expectation to perform well on the court, and there is perhaps doubt based on the spectacular nature of my fall. Vin Jr. handles all of this with a quiet dignity that I admire enormously. But I remind him and my other children often that I am happy just to be with them, and to be sharing in their journey. Every time I walk into a gym and see Vin or Kameron in a layup line I feel like I am in heaven already. After all, there were many years during which I didn't have that opportunity.

I don't waste time or energy fretting about what might have been, or what could have been. There are times I wish I hadn't blown all my money, of course, simply because I'd like to be able to do more for the people I love. But I don't lose sleep over it.

Money doesn't solve every problem. I was never sicker than when I was fabulously wealthy. Similarly, look at someone like Lamar Odom. Here's a kid with millions of dollars, with fame and talent and a beautiful spirit. A genuinely nice guy. But look where he wound up: comatose, stoned out of his mind, in the bedroom of a desert whorehouse. When I heard that news I was saddened beyond words. How lonely and depressed do you have to be to go out like that? Vegas isn't dark and depraved enough? You have to drive deep into the desert night, to a place called the Love Ranch, in order to meet your basest needs? I can imagine the pain in Lamar's heart, because, as they say . . .

There but for the Grace of God go I . . .

A lot of people who hear my story just don't understand. I'm not bitter. I am happy. I am filled with gratitude. I feel like I got a second chance in life, and no amount of money could have bought that. There are people who have incredible monetary wealth who still trudge through each day in a fog of delusion or depression. They didn't have the revelation that I had: that life isn't about material possessions. The Bible says it, and I know it to be true. I know this in my spirit: "What profits a man if he gains the whole world but loses his own soul?"

When I lost everything, it was like, *I gotta get my soul back. There's nothing else.* So I really believe that going broke was a blessing. Not a blessing in disguise, but an outright blessing. Losing all my money absolutely allowed me to stay alive. There is no question about it. I've told people that if I had $10 million in the bank when I was drinking myself to death, I can't promise that I would be here now. When the money dried up, I hit bottom, and I had to hit bottom in order to get better. I know what matters now: family, spirituality, health, kindness. It's a simpler life that I lead now, and I can say unequivocally that it is also a better life. A life that revolves around my church and my ministry, and the people I love.

It's taken a long time to rebuild my life and my reputation—years of concerted energy and effort (because talk is easy and empty; deeds matter). When word got out that I was working at Starbucks, there was a squall of publicity. I think a lot of people wondered what had become of me. It was almost like I had come back from the dead. The news that a former NBA all-star was working behind the counter at a coffee shop at first elicited sadness and pity . . . but then something else entirely. Approval, perhaps, or even . . . admiration. We all want to believe that we can overcome adversity, that there is the potential for redemption. Me? I was just trying to do a job to the best of my ability, and to be worthy of the opportunity that had been presented to me. But I noticed in the months after I began working for Starbucks that other doors began to open, doors that had been closed for a very long time. There were opportunities to speak with youth groups, and with men's groups, about issues ranging from substance abuse to leadership to the importance of fatherhood and what that word means in today's culture.

And then there was basketball.

I still love the game and believe that I have something to offer beyond coaching at the youth level or playing in alumni events, and I sense that I may not be the only one who feels that way. I've been getting more opportunities to consult with NBA teams, speaking to young players about financial issues and substance abuse. It's one thing for the coach or GM to stand up and talk to kids about these issues; it's quite another when they hear it from me. I can tell them that the money won't last forever, I can tell them that it is possible to go broke. I can look a nineteen-year-old rookie in the eye and say, "Son, I know you think you don't have a problem with weed, but I was the same way. And look where it got me."

Maybe they listen, maybe they don't. But I think the message resonates more coming from someone who has lived through it.

I like being around the game. I like teaching. And I think I'm pretty good at it. Which is why, in May 2016, I took a leave of absence from Starbucks. My consulting work had become more time consuming, and the NBA had just offered me a spot in its mentoring program for young, aspiring coaches. Basically, this was an opportunity—with the backing of the league—to hone my coaching skills in an effort to become more appealing as a candidate for a full-time job in the NBA. Shortly thereafter I got a call from the Milwaukee Bucks, who again asked me to coach their summer-league team in Las Vegas. I accepted the offer. Whether this would lead to a full-time position with the organization was difficult to say; I had received strong evaluations through the mentoring program and good feedback around the league. There were opportunities for coaching, player development, front office work, and broadcasting with any number of teams. I was open to all possibilities.

When I first made the decision to leave Starbucks, I did so with a bit of trepidation and guilt, but after speaking with Howard Schultz and realizing that I had his full support ("You belong in basketball, Vinnie"), I felt confident and peaceful. I wasn't turning my back on Howard or the company that practically saved my life. I was doing what I was meant to do, what I love to do, and what Starbucks helped make possible. If things didn't work out, Howard promised, I could always go back. Now was the right time to take a chance, in part because I could begin accessing my NBA pension, which would seriously lessen the financial anxiety and risk associated with changing career paths. You see, I'm not reckless—not anymore. I'm just passionate.

When summer league ended, I had a conversation with Peter Feigin, the president of the Milwaukee Bucks. He knew I was disappointed at not being offered a full-time coaching position.

"Don't worry, Vin," he said. "We have a plan for you."

Sure enough, in late September, I was offered a position as a television analyst with Fox Sports Wisconsin, a broadcast partner of the Bucks. My job was to offer pregame and post-game perspective for a select number of home games. It was an opportunity to be part of a professional broadcast team; equally important, it was a chance to get back in the arena on a regular basis, to let people know that I hadn't dropped off the face of the planet. I was healthy and happy. I was eager to work. And I was home, back in Milwaukee, where my professional career had begun.

One day in December I was sitting courtside at the Bucks' beautiful new training facility at North Sixth Street and West Juneau Avenue, watching the team run through practice, when I spotted a familiar figure walking toward me. Tall and lean, with a glistening, shaved head and expressive eyes, Kevin Garnett looked almost exactly as he had when we were teammates on the US Olympic team so many years earlier. Kevin had retired after the 2015–16 season following a long and illustrious NBA career, and he was now in the process of getting a consulting business off the ground. He had come to Milwaukee to speak with some of the team's younger players.

I couldn't tell if he saw me. It had been years since we had spoken, maybe as much as a decade. He walked all the way to the end of the gym, leaned against a wall, and watched practice with the same focus and intensity that had marked his playing career. I decided to walk over and say hello. As I got closer, I could see Kevin's eyes widening. And then he smiled.

"What's up, Kev?" I said. "How you been?"

Kevin shook his head in disbelief. "Holy shit, bro. I swear to God, I thought you were a ghost. Like, 'Am I looking at the ghost of Vin Baker?'"

"Nah, man. It's really me."

"You look good," he said.

"Thanks. I feel good."

A few minutes later, Jason Kidd walked over. We all hugged. The three of us had been teammates on the 2000 Olympic team. A lifetime ago.

"Look at you two," Jason said with a laugh. "Like old times."

That's the way it's been—a slow and organic resurrection, with one opportunity leading to another. In February, my broadcasting duties ended and I took an assistant coaching position with the Texas Legends of the NBA Development League. It's an apprenticeship through the league's mentoring program, and it could lead to a full-time coaching job down the road. I love being back in the game, working with young players in practice. In some ways, I have more energy now than I did when I was a player. I see things differently—on and off the court—and I want to share that vision, that experience, with others.

I don't know where the journey will take me next, but I have faith. I can feel in my bones that this is the right thing to do. I believe in my heart that basketball will provide a platform for not only taking care of my family and teaching the game I love, but also serving God and my community. Where this will all lead, I have no idea. But I feel good. I feel strong. After years of wandering aimlessly, so lost I thought I'd never find my way, this feels like the next righteous step on a sturdy and meaningful path.

ACKNOWLEDGMENTS

This is the place where I get to thank some of the people who not only made it possible for me to tell my life story but helped me have a life worth living.

My wife, Shawnee Baker, and our children, Vin Jr., Sanai, Kameron, and Aria.

My father, Pastor James Baker, and my mother, Jean Baker. And my brother, James, who passed away before I came along.

My grandmother Ada Richardson, and my uncles, Leroy Richardson and Robert Lee Baker. And my "partner in Christ," the Reverend O'Brien.

My father-in-law, Rich Pagan, and my mother-in-law, Linda Pagan.

Howard Schultz, who believed in me when almost no one else did, and who expected even more from me than I did from myself; Sheri Schultz, Jordan Schultz, Addi Schultz, and the entire Starbucks family, including Dan Pitasky, Scott Pitasky, and Peter Torrebiarte.

Dr. Calvin Butts and everyone at Abyssinian Baptist Church.

From the basketball world, past and present: Michael Jordan (who believed in me enough to give me my own signature shoe), Gary Payton, George Karl, Butch Carter, Mike Bond, Paul Spence, Rory Sparrow, Charlie Rosenzweig, Charles Smith, James Dolan, Artie Bayes, and the entire staff of the New York Knicks.

Special thanks to the Milwaukee Bucks for their support then and now, including Jason Kidd, Greg Foster, Peter Feigin, and Mike McCarthy, and the entire coaching staff.

Bishop T. D. Jakes, an inspiration in so many ways.

R. J., Meegan, and Olivia Bunch.

All of my extended family on both sides: the Bakers and the Richardsons.

Full Gospel Tabernacle Church, which nurtured me as a boy and continues to nurture me even now.

Old Saybrook High School and the University of Hartford.

My cousins, June and Diane Stallings. Ron and Gina Moye. Larry, Jay, and Donna Gillman. Deacon and Deaconess Jeffries. Bishop and Laurie Burgess. Jabarri Reynolds and Randye Rand.

Terry and David Bussie. Rogers Healy and Charli. Coach Girg.

And finally, to the people who helped make this book possible: my agent, Frank Weimann; my co-author, Joe Layden; our editor, Tracy Sherrod; and everyone at Amistad Press and HarperCollins.

ABOUT THE AUTHOR

Vin Baker spent thirteen years in the NBA, including four as an all-star. A graduate of the University of Hartford, where he remains the school's career leader in points and rebounds, he won a gold medal playing for the US Olympic team in 2000 and was selected by the Milwaukee Bucks as the eighth pick in the 1993 NBA draft. He is an assistant pastor and youth minister in his hometown of Old Saybrook, Connecticut. He also works as a consultant for the New York Knicks and is a member of the Professional Basketball Alumni Association. Baker lives in Old Saybrook with his family.